Altogether Now

*Essays on
Poetry,
Writing,
and Teaching*

Also by Chuck Guilford

Beginning College Writing
Nonfiction; Little, Brown and Company

What Counts
Poetry; Limberlost Press

Paradigm Online Writing Assistant
Nonfiction; Wordcurrent Press

Spring Drive: A North Country Tale
Fiction; Wordcurrent Press

Altogether Now

Essays on Poetry, Writing, and Teaching

by

Chuck Guilford

Wordcurrent Press

www.wordcurrent.com

First Wordcurrent Edition, September 2011

Copyright © 2011 by Chuck Guilford

Published in the United States
by Wordcurrent Press
www.wordcurrent.com

ISBN: 978-0-615-40889-7

Library of Congress Control Number (LCCN): 2011912945

Contents

Foreword

This book collects several articles, talks, and essays written over my academic career—a 30-year span—and includes pieces intended for both general and academic audiences. In preparing them for this collection, I've rethought and revised their style and substance.

Though the subjects range widely, if pressed to identify a common thread, I would say that they all celebrate the beauty and power of words, the power of language. A friend, and mutual admirer of the poet William Stafford, once said that many of Stafford's deepest and most meaningful experiences involved reading and writing. We looked at each other and smiled as though to say, "Yeah, I can relate."

"Back in the Classroom," the first piece, looks at how I got caught up in this profession and why I continue to labor in the vineyards even after retiring. As confused, rebellious, and stubborn as any teenager, I disliked much about school, but mostly the sense of regimentation, of being molded into W. H. Auden's "unknown citizen"— or even worse, Frank Stark, as played by Jim Backus in *Rebel Without a Cause*.

> Though the subjects range widely, if pressed to identify a common thread, I would say that they all celebrate the beauty and power of words, the power of language.

Growing up in Michigan, I was often "at risk," in school and out. Nevertheless, I loved to read and was fortunate to have many talented and caring teachers who changed my life more than they will ever know. Most, but not all, were English teachers. A biology teacher, Lucille Paslay, taught me more about life and learning than was in the curriculum, and a Sunday school teacher, John Gilray, ignited a curiosity about issues of faith and ultimate purpose that remains unextinguished after more than 50 years. This collection is dedicated to all of them—too many to list here. And especially to my friends and family for their patience, support, encouragement, and love.

"Words, words, words," said Hamlet, pacing the stage, himself a creation of words built by Shakespeare's imagination from bits of fact and legend, those pieces themselves made of words—patterns of sound representing some human awareness encoded in written characters—printed and read, spoken and heard. Words and language, these have been my chosen tools for exploring issues and questions raised so many years ago. And I may have found some answers, but the greatest rewards have come in the process of discovery.

How is it that our days
come down to this

perpetual present
like a vanishing storm

until for an instant
each gesture is sacred

each small sound an echo
in a temple of bone?

Back in the Classroom

As a child, I never dreamed of being a teacher, never even imagined I might become one. That's not to say I had any aversion to teaching, just that compared to playing professional baseball, writing best-selling novels, or working at the corner gas station, such a career didn't look attractive.

I mean, did you ever see kids collect bubble gum cards with pictures of teachers on them? Would Mrs. Briggs, my long-suffering geometry teacher, ever see her lesson on the Pythagorean theorem made into a major motion picture starring Natalie Wood and Kirk Douglas? What teacher could install dual quads in a custom '32 Ford roadster, then open the soft drink machine and offer a free orange soda to a gawking 13-year-old boy?

> Certainly, at 16, I would have said that I learned more from Woodward Avenue than I ever did from a teacher.

Wally Bitterle could do that. He was a mechanic at the corner Speedway 79 station. Bruce Springsteen would have written a song about that car if he'd seen it peel out of Maverick Drive-In onto Woodward Avenue, vanishing into the night through a veil of thin blue smoke, leaving behind just the smell of burnt rubber.

Springsteen once claimed that he learned more from a three-minute record than he ever learned in school. I think I know what he meant. Certainly, at 16, I would have said that I learned as much from Woodward Avenue as I ever did in a classroom.

In the world of Woodward Avenue, teachers did not exist. They had their own world—the world of school, a kind of self-contained, separate reality. Though I understood even then that teachers left school at day's end and went home like other people, some to wives or husbands, others, even more remarkably, to children, I seldom saw them "off the grounds."

If I did bump into a teacher, say at Quarton Market or the Mills Pharmacy, I would immediately revert to school behavior—no more laughing or talking, watch the grammar, try to look interested but avoid all eye contact. Once the encounter was over, a cloud had passed. My mood grew warm and light. I might peel the paper from a fresh toothpick, slip that wooden stick between my lips and savor its minty taste as I shredded the sharp tip between my teeth.

> What I loved most about those lines, more even than their riddling irony, was their bold and beautiful ungrammaticality.

Teachers liked toothpicks even less than they liked short pants. Shorts took our minds off our studies and focused them on the human anatomy. Toothpicks, I supposed, were considered dangerous. "That could put somene's eye out. You'd better leave it with me. I'll keep it here in my desk with my collection of combs, nail files, and Bazooka gum."

Away from school, relishing my freedom, I'd hum a few bars of my favorite Chuck Berry song:

Back in the classroom, open the books.
Even the teacher don't know how mean she looks.

What I loved most about those lines, more even than their riddling irony, was their bold and beautiful ungrammaticality. They were so un-school, so gloriously superior to the whole drab institution. Chuck Berry reminded me of Huck Finn. I liked their attitudes.

I learned about Chuck Berry from Rockin' Robin Seymour, a disc jockey on WKMH in Detroit. I learned about Huck Finn from Mrs. Kinnison, my eleventh grade English teacher. She liked Huck, too, I could tell. And that sort of puzzled me, what with Huck being like he was, somewhat less than a model student. Mrs. Kinnison was supposed to like Tom Sawyer's well-behaved brother, Sid. Nevertheless, Huck and Jim and I floated down the Mississippi along with Mrs. Kinnison and about 20 other kids.

Together, we slit a pig's throat and spread its blood around Pap's cabin. We entered the big frame house that floated downriver, the one with the mysterious corpse that spooked Jim so. We listened as Jim told about how he hit his daughter 'Lizabeth one time for not shutting the door, then realized she had just gone deaf.

Mrs. Kinnison*—Mrs. K, I had come to call her—had a way of making us feel right there in the novel, trying to figure out why the characters acted the way they did. Why did Huck treat Jim like a child when Jim was the adult? Was this a sign of prejudice? How could that be? Huck and Jim were friends. Huck wasn't prejudiced. "Why don't we look up 'prejudice'?" she might say.

> We entered the big frame house that floated downriver, the one with the mysterious corpse that spooked Jim so.

This could lead to a broader discussion of whether there was such a thing as unconscious prejudice and a debate on whether racial tension could be a good thing if it eventually brought greater awareness of social injustice. Such debates were spirited, sometimes intensely emotional, and feeling my adrenalin flow, I joined in eagerly, often taking a stand less on the basis of personal conviction than on the chance of teasing out new thoughts and further discussion.

* Betty Kinnison, a truly gifted teacher, is used here in part to represent the many generous, inspired, brilliant teachers I have been blessed with at all levels of my education.

"How," I might wonder aloud, "can anyone in this class even claim to like Huck at all? He's a liar, a hypocrite, a coward and a social misfit. He's not even very smart, yet everyone talks about him like he was the all-American boy. Heck, Mrs. K would have kicked him out of class the first week." Of course I didn't believe that last part. Mrs. K was no mean teacher. In fact, she was starting to remind me of the Widow Douglas.

> "Well, Huck," I imagine her saying, "if you think getting civilized means having your spirit broken and becoming a mindless conformist, you're sadly mistaken.

"Well, Huck," I imagine her saying, "if you think getting civilized means having your spirit broken and becoming a mindless conformist, you're sadly mistaken. On the contrary, it was the Persians, whom the Greeks called 'Barbarians,' who were the prisoners of their own fear and ignorance. But in Athens, individuality flourished. Study Aristophanes, Huck. Read Plato."

"This Socrates guy," Huck might say a week later, "Tom says they killed him just fer speakin' his mind. He says they had slavery in Athens. Now if that ain't the civilized way!" Huck would think he had scored a point, but Mrs. K. would know she had him hooked. He was reading. He was thinking. Just as I was getting hooked, and not only on reading or Betty Kinnison.

I wanted to write books, but not just best-sellers. I wanted to write like Mark Twain or Charles Dickens or J. D. Salinger or Albert Camus. My books would transform people's lives, shape the future of the planet. People would get lost in them for weeks at a time and emerge wiser, stronger, more fulfilled. I also wanted to learn . . . something. I wasn't sure what. I needed guidance and direction—teachers, more than high school could offer. And I needed people to discuss and debate with—college students and then graduate students.

I still need these things, which may explain why 40 years later I'm still in school. Now, though, after years as a student, I walk to the front of the room, step behind the lectern and sort through my notes, watching a last few reluctant learners claim seats in the room's far corners.

I've obviously become a teacher, but this becoming happened gradually, almost unconsciously as I moved from student to teaching assistant to professor. Even now, I eagerly shift roles as I ask students to explain how their writing influences their thinking, or ask them to teach me what Wordsworth means in "Tintern Abbey" when he speaks of "something far more deeply interfused / Whose dwelling is the light of setting suns." More deeply infused than what? Why is "suns" plural?—I want to know.

> Because I see how much I still have to learn, even in areas that are my specialties, I keep asking and answering questions.

Because I see how much I still have to learn, even in areas that are my specialties, I keep asking and answering questions. And because I see this same hunger in so many of my students, I want to offer them help and support. Being a university professor permits me to do these things, which I enjoy immensely and believe to be worthwhile, though I no longer dream of seeing my picture on a bubble gum card, and my achievements with automobile engines over the years have seldom gone beyond jumping dead batteries.

These days, I do still write—poetry, essays, fiction. But my dreams of literary fame have been tempered by a sobering recognition of what I can reasonably hope to accomplish. And each year I find growing satisfaction in teaching, in the thought that I may be as helpful to some of my students as Mrs. Kinnison, and so many others, have been to me.

Dreams of Paradise and Light:
Henry Vaughan's Metaphysical Quest

Henry Vaughan lived in Wales in the mid 1600s and wrote in a poetic tradition that stressed correspondence and harmony, that saw the universe as a manifestation of the mind of God, a book of nature, written in metaphor, image, and symbol. Yet he lived in a time of shifting paradigms when philosophical skepticism, scientific discovery, and civil war shook the foundations upon which that vision of correspondence and unity had been based.

The seventeenth century was a time of intellectual upheaval when long-established beliefs were unsettled by the astronomy of Copernicus, the optics of Galilleo, the skepticism of Montaigne, the dualism of Descartes, the empiricism of Bacon. More and more, a split was opening between faith and reason. Whereas for centuries no distinction had been made between a religious truth and a scientific fact, now, in a way that T. S. Eliot famously called a "dissociation of sensibility," the truths of religion, based on faith and applicable to the spiritual realm, and the truths of science, based on reason and applicable to the physical realm, were heading in separate directions.

> More and more, a split was opening between faith and reason.

Confronted with this disconnect between a Renaissance vision of divine harmony and the antithetical new ideas that threatened it, Vaughan and the other "metaphysical poets"—John Donne and George Herbert especially—concluded that dissociation and discord were not fundamental to the world, but rather the result of wrong thinking, of humanity's alienation from God, an alienation that fostered a despiritualized, fragmented, and consequently imperfect world view.

The metaphysical poets, however, struggled to reassert and redefine the essential unity of the spiritual and the physical realms. A basic assumption of these poets is not only that this unity exists, but also that their poems should demonstrate a harmony of correspondence and interrelationship embracing even the most apparently dissociated phenomena. In Vaughan's poems especially, the spiritual and physical realms are so bound up with the imagination, and spiritual imperfection so involved with physical imperfection that precise distinctions among spirit, mind, and matter are, at best, difficult to make.

...the consequence of the Fall is the divided self in which a spiritual soul is at odds with a physical body.

In the quest for truth and wholeness, the individual, rather than the physical world, had to be transformed, and with that transformation, the physical world's apparent imperfections would no longer exist. What this amounts to is a recognition of the psychological commonplace that our judgments about the external world are often projections of our own psyches. Or in Christian terms, the consequence of the Fall is the divided self in which a spiritual soul is at odds with a physical body. Humans see themselves as having a dual nature and project this duality onto the external world.

As a physician in Brecon, Wales, Vaughan might have been expected to cast his lot with Francis Bacon and the "new men" of science, but that was not his way. Instead, he chose the path of Hermetic medicine, an ancient tradition related to alchemy, in which the mind mediates between the spiritual and the physical realms. It receives influence from the spiritual and makes this influence operable on the physical level, thus healing the sick and also allowing the transformation of base metals to gold. As Carl Jung puts it,

Alchemy set itself the task of acquiring this "treasure hard to attain" and of producing it in visible form as the physical gold or the panacea or the transforming tincture—in so far as the art still busied itself in the laboratory. But since the practical work was never quite free of the unconscious contents of the operator which found expression in it, it was, at the same time a psychic activity which can best be compared to what we call the active imagination. (345-46)

For a Hermetic physician like Vaughan, each herb or flower had a unique blend of spritual and physical properties, was infused with a divine spark or signature that gave it healing power. The physician had to be spiritually pure in order to select and administer specific herbs and remedies that could heal patients holistically, body and spirit. In this process, the spiritual and the physical aspects of healing finally became inseparable.

As a poet, also, Vaughan sought to recover a unified vision and to show that fragmentation and discord were errors of understanding resulting from moral imperfection. Poetic imagination became a way to reassert the spiritual unity of the physical world by demonstrating correspondence and sympathy. Metaphysical wit sought to prove that a right-thinking intellect could see beyond the apparent fragmentation of the world and rediscover the essential unity that had been obscured by humanity's growing alienation from God.

In his famous letter to Arthur Johnson, William Drummond of Hawthornden first used the term "metaphysical" with reference to Donne and his followers:

> The physician had to be spiritually pure in order to select and administer specific herbs and remedies that could heal patients holistically.

*In vain have some Men of late (Transformers of every Thing)
consulted upon her [poetry's] Reformation, and endeavoured
to abstract her to metaphysical Ideas, and Scholastical
Quiddities, denuding her of her own Habits, and those
ornaments with which she hath amused the whole World some
Thousand Years. (143)*

While Drummond's description of these poets as metaphysical
is often noted, his reference to them
as "Transformers of every Thing"
does not receive as much attention.
The desire to imaginatively
transform the physical world,
however, is at heart of metaphysical
poetry. In fact, the intellectual
tension of metaphysical wit stems
largely from the poets' attempts to
respiritualize the physical world.
That is, within the lines of a poem,
these poets sought to eliminate
discord and fragmentation by
integrating the apparently disconnected components of
their experience into a spiritually unified whole.

Although this transformation is *imaginative*, we
would be wrong to see it as merely *imaginary*, the entire
point being to show that dissociation rather than unity
is illusory. Because the illusion of dissociation results
from moral apostasy (originally the Fall from Eden)
the illusion can be eliminated only by first purging
the self of impurity, to recover spiritual wholeness.
Thus, the transformation of the world depends on the
transformation of the self to a state in which the individual
sees the world from a meta-perspective, where even the
"husks and shells of things" are aspects of an all-embracing
oneness.

For Vaughan childhood represents a stage in the *microcosm* that is equivalent to the Edenic age of the *macrocosm*. Only by recovering the purity of unfallen Adam and Eve can humans hope to eliminate the dissociation and discord that envelop unregenerate adults. Vaughan sees the state of fallen mankind as analogous to the *Old Testament* covenant of Hebraic Law, a dark time when the only spiritual illumination received by humans came from stars, and even the stars were frequently obscured by mists and clouds. Christ is the regenerative force, the Sun, which offers a way out of that darkness. In Christ, we are offered the chance to be reborn, and to live in the light is to regain the spiritual wholeness of a child. But first "the old self must die."

> Dissociation and fragmentation occur only when we fail to see the world from this divine perspective—when we introduce separation and opposition.

Marriage to Christ, thus, represents the regeneration and transformation of humanity, as individual will and divine will, individual vision and divine vision merge into one. Just as transformation of the microcosm requires that the individual cease to exist as something apart from God, so transformation of the macrocosm demands that every aspect of experience be consumed by the all-subduing might of God. That is, the individual must realize that the created world is a manifestation of the Divine Mind and see that in that Mind all things are One. Dissociation and fragmentation occur only when we fail to see the world from this divine perspective—when we introduce separation and opposition.

The quest for transformation, then, amounts to a quest for mystical union with God and is analogous to the Hermetic *opus*, which sought to produce the *elixir*, or philosopher's stone. Vaughan's Hermetic imagery works with his other quest imagery to lend a rich layer of secondary associations to his account of his own struggle for transformation. Christ becomes the *lapis* or the *balm* that transforms us to our original, incorruptible state and grants us eternal life. He is the *transforming tincture* that removes all grossness of matter, making us pure and incorruptible. He allows us to imaginatively transform the macrocosm, by eliminating all opposition and discord.

Because alchemical symbols represent stages in a process, the language of Hermeticism is well-suited to a description of the mystic's quest. Thus, the *Prima Materia*, or primary matter, in which *nous* and *physis* are one, is equivalent to the Edenic unity of unfallen humanity. The separation of spirit from secondary, corruptible matter is equivalent to the state of mankind after the Fall. Here the seed, or the divine spark (in humans, the soul), sleeps imprisoned in gross matter (the body). This is the state of fallen humanity, whom Vaughan frequently describes as being a ward or in bondage. The alchemist putrefies base matter in an alembic, extracting the elixir, or philosophers' stone, which allows the chymist then to purge metals of their grossness or the physician to heal the infirmities of a patient.* This, of course, is a simplification of a complex and obscure process,

> The images with which Vaughan describes his quest for spiritual transformation become actual proofs of his success or failure in reaching his goal.

---

*See Mazzeo, Joseph Anthony. *Renaissance and Seventeenth Century Studies* (New York; Columbia Universlty Press, 1954), pp. 77-79, for a brief and lucid explanation of how the transformatlve process was performed.

but it shows how Hermetic imagery works with the more conventional Christian imagery used by Vaughan to describe his quest for transformation and unity.

Since the intent of metaphysical imagery was both to *assert* and to *demonstrate* the mind's ability to uncover a divine unity in the physical world, Vaughan's use of the poem as an alembic most clearly places him in the metaphysical tradition. The images with which Vaughan describes his quest for spiritual transformation become actual proofs of his success or failure

> The poem is a beautifully wrought and surprisingly complex account of Vaughan's own quest for unity.

in reaching his goal. His use of correspondence is not just ornamental, but marks his progress toward that final unity in which all the limitations and illusions of apostate man vanish in the pure light of God. The poem itself becomes an alembic where the fragmentation and limitation of gross, secondary matter are putrefied in the heat of the right thinking intellect so that the transforming elixir is released, wholly regenerating and perfecting both the microcosm and the macrocosm.

In "Cock-Crowing" Vaughan's imagery shows this transformative process at work. The poem is a beautifully wrought and surprisingly complex account of the poet's vision quest. At the same time, it shows through its interweaving of orthodox religious, natural, and Hermetic imagery how he sought to achieve this transformation:

> *Father of lights! what sunny seed,*
> *What glance of day hast Thou confined*
> *Into this bird? To all the breed*
> *This busy ray Thou hast assigned;*

Opening with an apostrophe to the "Father of lights," Vaughan immediately starts developing two of the poem's central themes—influence and correspondence. The bird contains a "Sunnie seed" or a "glance of day," the divine spark that, as Elizabeth Holmes points out (38), creates influence and accounts for the cock's peculiar attraction to dawn. Although the spark is "confin'd" or imprisoned within the bird, it works like a magnet seeking out the greater light of God from whence it came:

> *Their magnitism works all night,*
> *And dreams of paradise and light.*

"Night" suggests alienation from the light. The cock, longing for the sun, corresponds to Old Testament humanity awaiting the arrival of the Son of God, and also to Vaughan himself, awaiting transformation in Christ. Thus, Vaughan sets up the pattern of the poem. The "glance of day," temporarily alienated from its source and imprisoned in gross matter, seeks liberation and unity. As M. M. Mahood says, speaking of the poem:

> The "glance of day," temporarily alienated from its source and imprisoned in gross matter, seeks liberation and unity.

> *We have already seen that when Thomas Vaughan* [the poet's brother] *writes about the Philosopher's Stone, he means a transmutation of the soul; the highest alchemy is such a revelation of the First Matter as consists in freeing the heart from all material impurities, and thus preparing it for that secret incubation of the spirit of God whereby the spiritual elements of the mind are reunited with their heavenly counterparts. (282)*

The poem represents precisely this process. But it would be wrong to see the cock as merely an allegorical figure. Vaughan is not just using the cock to make a parallel; he is using it to show how the right-thinking mind illuminates the physical world by revealing order and eliminating apparent dissociation.

The third stanza, as Don Cameron Allen points out, contrasts the cock's *sapentia* with human *intelligentia* (165). The image of God is capable of greater feats than the cock, but at the same time, humans can choose darkness over light. We can extinguish the divine spark and let the seed of divinity wither:

> *To sleep without Thee is to die;*
> *Yea, 'tis a death partakes of hell:*
> *For where Thou dost not close the eye,*
> *It never opens, I can tell.*
>   *In such a dark Egyptian border,*
>   *The shades of death dwell, and disorder.*

Death and disorder result from our failure to nurture the seed of divinity, refusing "To watch for thy appearing hour." They are the results of abandoning our quest for the transforming elixir. Vaughan's reference to the "dark Aegyptian border" alludes to the curse of darkness cast by Moses upon the Egyptians, who had refused to let Moses and his people leave, and is, thus, deeper than the darkness of the Israelites, who were the Lord's chosen people. It is the barren ignorance of those who refuse to accept divine wisdom.

Yet, conscious of the seed that abides in him, Vaughan rejects death and disorder for the "immortal Light and Heat" of God:

> *Seeing thy seed abides In me,*
> *Dwell thou in it, and I in thee.*

The correspondences beautifully merge in the lines:

Whose hand so shines through all this frame,
That by the beauty of the seat,
We plainly see, who made the same.

The phrase, "this frame," refers most immediately to the macrocosm, but it also refers to the bird and to Vaughan, all of which can be transformed by the pure light of Christ, and all of which, rightly seen, reveal the glory of God.

Still, sensing that his transformation is incomplete, Vaughan longs to move beyond mere "gleams and fractions" of divine vision. He sees that, despite his awareness of order and correspondence, he has not found the transforming elixir which would, as he puts it in "They Are All Gone into the World of Light," "Resume thy spirit from the world of thrall / Into true liberty." His final transformation is denied by the cloak of his own mortal limitation, which obstructs his vision of God and imprisons his soul:

Only this veil which Thou hast broke,
And must be broken yet in me,
This veil, I say, is all the cloak
And cloud which shadows Thee from me.
*   This veil Thy full-eyed love denies,*
*   And only gleams and fractions spies.*

The veil was removed by Christ, who redeemed the macrocosm from death and darkness, but Vaughan understands that this same process must take place in each person. He must shake off the darkness of his own imperfection and liberate his soul from its bondage:

O take it off! make no delay;
But brush me with Thy light that I

May shine unto a perfect day,
And warm me at Thy glorious eye!
* O take it off, or till it flee,*
* Though with no lily, stay with me!*

Only when the soul is released from confinement does it "shine unto a perfect day," eliminating all illusion of duality. In this state, when all duality has been purged and the human mind is united with the mind of God, dissociation and imperfection vanish. The individual spark is finally reunited with the Sun, and as we see the world through the "glorious Eye" of God, the transformation is complete.

> Only when the soul is released from confinement does it "shine unto a perfect day," eliminating all illusion of duality.

In this poem, however, as in so many others, Vaughan's awareness of his own shortcomings prevents the final union he so ardently desired. Nevertheless, despite his failures to achieve that final holistic unity, his poetry remains a powerful and moving record of his quest. Lacking the sheer power and force of Donne's intellect or the careful control of Herbert's poetic craftsmanship, Vaughan's poems are filled with moments of enthusiasm, quiet reverence, and brooding melancholy. And always there is hope. If Vaughan sometimes lacks faith in mankind, he never loses faith in the redemptive power of Christ.

Perhaps it is in this personal sense that the twenty-first century reader can most relate to Henry Vaughan, whose tenacious imagination is always at the center of the poem, struggling to achieve a unified vision of the spiritual and physical realms. Certainly a full appreciation of all the nuances of Vaughan's poetry requires acquaintance with intellectual traditions that are not part of a modern reader's general store of knowledge. Yet, while a full study of these sources is beyond the scope of this essay, I hope I have shown how the imagery and structure of the poems reveal both a general vision of the world that Vaughan shared with many of his contemporaries and a personal vision which, because it was so largely defined by the unique terms in which Vaughan expressed it, remains a strikingly original poetic achievement.

Works Cited

Allen, Don Cameron. *Image and Meaning.* Baltimore: The Johns Hopkins Press, 1960.

Drummond, William of Hawthornden. *The Works of Drummond of Hawthornden.* Edinburgh, 1711.

Holmes, Elizabeth. *Henry Vaughan and the Hermetic Philosophy,* 1932; rpt. New York: Russell & Russell, 1967.

Jung, Carl G. *Psychology and Alchemy.* Trans. R. C. F. Hull. 2nd. ed. Bollingen Series, Vol 20. Princeton: Princeton Unniversity Press, 1968.

Mahood, M. M. *Poetry and Humanism.* New Haven: Yale University Press, 1950.

Cock-Crowing

by Henry Vaughan (1621-1695)

Father of lights! what sunny seed,
What glance of day hast Thou confined
Into this bird? To all the breed
This busy ray Thou hast assigned;
    Their magnetism works all night,
    And dreams of paradise and light.

Their eyes watch for the morning hue;
Their little grain, expelling night,
So shines and sings as if it knew
The path unto the house of light.
    It seems their candle, howe'er done,
    Was tinned and lighted at the sun.

If such a tincture, such a touch,
So firm a longing can empower,
Shall Thy own image think it much
To watch for Thy appearing hour?
    If a mere blast so fill the sail,
    Shall not the breath of God prevail?

O Thou immortal Light and Heat!
Whose hand so shines through all this frame
That, by the beauty of the seat,
We plainly see who made the same,
    Seeing Thy seed abides in me,
    Dwell Thou in it, and I in Thee!

To sleep without Thee is to die;
Yea, 'tis a death partakes of hell:
For where Thou dost not close the eye,
It never opens, I can tell.
    In such a dark Egyptian border,
    The shades of death dwell, and disorder.

If joys, and hopes, and earnest throes,
And hearts whose pulse beats still for light
Are given to birds, who but Thee knows
A love-sick soul's exalted flight?
    Can souls be tracked by any eye
    But His who gave them wings to fly?

Only this veil which Thou hast broke,
And must be broken yet in me,
This veil, I say, is all the cloak
And cloud which shadows Thee from me.
    This veil Thy full-eyed love denies,
    And only gleams and fractions spies.

O take it off! make no delay;
But brush me with Thy light that I
May shine unto a perfect day,
And warm me at Thy glorious eye!
    O take it off, or till it flee,
    Though with no lily, stay with me!

1655

Creating a Learning Flow for Exploratory Writing

Consider two ways of looking at writing. In the first, writing consists of recording known information, giving it order and permanence so it can be examined and understood by others. In the second, writing is a way of coming to know what is unfamiliar and of participating in an ongoing conversation with readers.

While most writing teachers are committed to the second view, my experience suggests that most writing students are wedded to the first. As teachers, we speak about "exploratory writing" and "writing to learn," but too many students resist writing until they feel certain not only of their thesis, but even their basic pattern of support and development. As a result, they tend to waver between debilitating anxiety about getting started on a project and premature closure of intellectual inquiry once they have begun.

> Frustrated by the difficulty of getting my students to see writing as an act of discovery, I realized that much of the problem was due to an inconsistency between my teaching goals and my teaching methods.

Frustrated by the difficulty of getting my students to see writing as an act of discovery, I realized that much of the problem was due to an inconsistency between my teaching goals and my teaching methods. I wanted to encourage students to use writing to inquire into unfamiliar and often intimidating subject areas, but the overall sequence and structure of classroom activities leading to completion of an essay was not designed to do this. For instance, students who couldn't get started on an assignment were encouraged to try free writing or mind mapping, but because these activities were not integrated into an overall experiential flow, they often proved only marginally helpful, sometimes providing useful ideas but frequently turning into dead ends or even distractions.

In order to align my goals and methods, I needed to make some major changes in the operation of the class, especially in my approach to writing assignments, which had been conceived of and presented largely as "outcomes expected" rather than as "projects to be undertaken." Even such a minor change as this had benefits in that it clearly emphasized the making of the writing as our central concern.

Thus, I found myself saying not, "On Monday you will get your next assignment," but "On Monday we will begin a new writing project." Nor was this just a name change, a distinction without a difference, for while I did continue to spell out the scope and purpose of the task ahead, I also explained that the exact nature of the final paper could not be known in advance but would emerge gradually as a result of decisions and discoveries made along the way. Moreover, individual students might proceed in very different directions, depending upon their personal interests and the constraints imposed by their specific rhetorical problems.

> I wanted to help them ease into the writing process while still in a state of uncertainty, and *use* that uncertainty as inspiration and motivation for the ongoing process of making meaning through writing.

In short, I wanted to help them ease into the writing process while still in a state of uncertainty, and *use* that uncertainty as inspiration and motivation for the ongoing process of making meaning through writing. The key word here is "help," for it is not enough simply to goad or exhort them; they need to be equipped to identify, explore, and resolve issues that they find genuinely problematic.

The following process is one that I have found can help students at various levels of ability use writing as a tool of investigation and problem solving.

I teach at an open admissions university and have used this method most extensively in my advanced writing courses, but have also found it effective, with minor adaptations, in freshman classes, especially during the second semester. It is based primarily upon a Piagetian learning cycle that asks students to identify areas of cognitive dissonance, to explore the sources of that dissonance, and to engage in a conversation (partly written and partly oral) about ways of resolving their uncertainty. Most of the individual activities, such as free writing or mind mapping, are familiar enough to require little explanation. Rather, I will consider some of the ways such activities can be used in an overall flow of learning and writing from the initiation of a writing project to its completion. In the interest of clarity, I will present the process in terms of stages, but these stages do not always have clear-cut beginnings and endings; they sometimes overlap and blend into each other. Also, they do not always proceed in a neat linear fashion, as writers often "leap ahead" to a later stage or "circle back" to revise earlier work.

> They need to get inside of the subject and to get the subject inside of them in a way they find truly meaningful.

Involvement and Interaction

During the earliest stages of a project, students need to develop an authentic personal involvement with their subject. They need to get inside of the subject and get the subject inside of them in a way they find truly meaningful. For instance, if they are writing on a series of related readings, they need to let go of preconceived notions about the proper or expected way of responding and instead to connect the reading material with their own world of experience and understanding.

In a recent class, we used a reader designed for an American studies program and containing readings organized by theme on such topics as Puritanism, the individual and society, and the problem of exclusion (Robert H. Fossum and John K. Roth, eds., *American Ground: Vistas, Visions & Revisions*, New York: Paragon House, 1988). Nonwriting activities during the early stages of a project on exclusion might consist of having small groups select passages from W. E. B. DuBois, Martin Luther King, or Adrienne Rich to be read aloud to the whole class. Or students might be asked to brainstorm questions about a particular reading—"Letter from Birmingham Jail," for instance—and compare questions with other members of a discussion group. Each group would then present several questions to the whole class. This is also a good time to make use of journals and other resources for informal, expressive writing. Students are encouraged to write subjective personal responses to passages that have been read aloud. I encourage them toward such responses as "This reminds me of …" or "This makes me feel …" or "I don't understand how …."

This is also a good time to make use of journals and other resources for informal, expressive writing.

In the unit on exclusion, for example, students wanted to know: What creates the "Veil" that DuBois mentions in "The Souls of Black Folk" and how does it influence perceptions between the races? Why does King consider the white moderates to be more of a problem than the racists? What justifications were given for putting Japanese-Americans in internment camps during WWII? Does Adrienne Rich think that men discriminate against women because they feel intimidated or threatened? As students clarify their own responses and compare these with their classmates', they get a sense of which issues matter to them personally and how their individual perspective fits into the overall mix of concerns expressed by the class.

Results of such sessions are generally quite chaotic. Sometimes a dominant pattern emerges, but more often a variety of perspectives comes to the surface, suggesting multiple possibilities for further investigation and exploration. If the subject is not drawn from readings, the same procedure can be used with only minor modifications. For instance, instead of selecting passages to be read aloud, students could give a detailed description of a scene from a film or could recount significant incidents or experiences relating to the subject. In any event, the goal is not to establish a comprehensive understanding of the subject or even to choose a topic to write on so much as to immerse themselves in the material in a way that has personal significance—to possess the subject and, conversely, allow the subject to possess them.

> Sometimes a dominant pattern emerges, but more often a variety of perspectives comes to the surface, suggesting multiple possibilities for further investigation and exploration.

Focus and Commitment

Precisely because the first stage tends to produce an unsystematic jumble of ideas and impressions that overlap and intersect in ways that may complement or contradict each other, it becomes necessary to start sorting things out. At this point, then, I encourage students to look for patterns in their earlier responses, to separate major concerns from minor ones, central issues from peripheral ones, and especially to consider which of the many points that have already been raised call for further discussion and more sustained examination.

A typical class activity might involve having each student make a list of three concerns ranked in order of interest. A question asking what W. E. B. DuBois' initials stand for would probably receive a low ranking, for instance. Students focus on a specific topic that they find personally engaging and are willing to explore more fully in their writing projects. Then without revealing the ranking, students discuss the individual lists in small groups, considering such matters as their level of personal commitment to an issue, the scope and importance of the issue, the availability of information on the subject, and the kinds of problems they would expect to encounter in writing about it. Finally, they reveal their original rankings and discuss whether they need to re-order their choices or perhaps clarify and refine their intentions so as to arrive at a workable topic. I make it clear that I am not looking for answers so much as questions, not solutions but problems. I want them to understand that we are a long way from needing a thesis and that, in fact, at this point a thesis may be more of a hindrance than a help, as it can create a false sense of certainty and prematurely shut down further inquiry.

> Students focus on a specific topic that they find personally engaging and are willing to explore more fully in their writing projects.

If, as is sometimes the case, a student has difficulty committing to a single focus, I try to help with the decision, not by giving my preference but by asking leading questions such as "Why do you want to write on sexual discrimination?" "Where would you find information on this?" "Are you more concerned with the causes or the effects of this issue?" "What related issues would you have to consider in order to examine the matter thoroughly?" The goal, finally, is for each student to identify a focus for further exploration and to make a commitment to pursuing the matter as the writing project continues to evolve.

Trying on Ideas

While to my mind the project is well under way by now, many students will not feel so comfortable. They can feel daunted by the prospect of writing about a subject they have not yet mastered. Besides reassuring them that their apprehensions are normal and healthy, I begin to show them how to systematically explore the issues they are working with. Class activities often involve working with the journalists' questions, the pentad, or tagmemics. Students may also find branching trees and mind maps helpful ways of identifying major divisions and understanding the relationship of parts to the whole and to each other.

Imagine a student who, as a result of interests aroused by reading and personal experience, is exploring the problem of unconscious sexism in her workplace.

Sensing a need for more information, some individuals may begin to research their topics online, in the library, or by conducting interviews or surveys. This is also a good time for more free writing, focused now on specific subtopics identified in the heuristic exercises. The free writes and the heuristic experiments are often shared informally in discussion groups so that class members can get suggestions about their own work and learn from the efforts of others.

Imagine a student who, as a result of interests aroused by reading and personal experience, is exploring the problem of unconscious sexism in her workplace. She may be asking where these attitudes come from; who holds them; how they have changed over time; how this sexism manifests itself; how it affects men, women, the overall atmosphere at work, the quality of work produced; how these attitudes can be exposed and overcome. She may be free writing about her own experiences, interviewing coworkers and supervisors, researching literature on the causes and effects of discrimination. She may find that she can apply the ideas of King or DuBois to her own situation. In class, she will share her ideas in a discussion group, continuing to look for patterns, implications, and new perspectives, while helping others to do the same with their topics.

> As such questions are answered, students feel an emerging sense of certainty and satisfaction, a tentative recognition of closure.

Without my suggesting it, she will almost certainly sense a need for order and system to her inquiry. She may need to do some further mind mapping, make an informal outline, or simply list important subpoints. Probably also, she will be looking for some sort of answer or solution to the overarching problem she has been exploring. She may not be ready to formulate this into a clear thesis, but will likely be moving in that direction.

Rather than encouraging her to reach for a thesis immediately, I might suggest trying out a few different possibilities so that their strengths and weaknesses can be examined. Does she believe these sexist attitudes are so deeply ingrained by cultural conditioning and the structure of the work environment that she can not hope to counteract them? Does she feel that increased social awareness of sexual discrimination may have created a climate in which she and other women at work can hope to change the status quo? Could she make use of King's four basic steps for a nonviolent campaign? What has she discovered in her inquiry that would lead her to favor one solution over another?

As such questions are answered, students feel an emerging sense of certainty and satisfaction, a tentative recognition of closure. To be sure, much work remains ahead, but most students will feel ready to float a trial thesis, and as they do, they will see how it can serve as an organizational and conceptual center for their essay.

Revising for Readers

Up to this point, most of the writing has been informal and expressive. If students have produced drafts at all, these are usually quite rough and will require significant revision on both the macro and micro levels. As a working draft is produced, mind maps, scratch outlines, and other organizational aids can be helpful in suggesting major divisions and even the placement of subpoints within those divisions, but unless an audience has been identified from the outset (and I can see both advantages and disadvantages of doing so), most writers will not have given much attention to the impact of their writing on projected readers. They will not have adequately considered the amounts and kinds of information that their readers want or need. They may not have thought much about the arrangement of the major points of their discussion, including the placement of their thesis. Should it come at the beginning or the end? Should it be directly stated or implied? And very few will have shown much concern for establishing a consistent rhetorical stance in terms of tone, voice, or degree of formality. This is where cutting and pasting, substituting and rewriting, begin in earnest.

> Up to this point, most of the writing has been informal and expressive.

Once students have produced a working draft, they can exchange copies with members of their discussion group or simply read the drafts aloud to the group. Sometimes students find it helpful to listen quietly while their draft is read aloud by another group member. Role playing can also be helpful here. Other group members, or even the writer if the paper is being read aloud by someone else, can try to anticipate possible responses of the audience, reacting to both style and substance. Does one idea flow naturally into another? Is the writer belaboring the obvious? Are examples and illustrations relevant and convincing? Does the voice sound authentic? Is the style too formal? Too chummy?

This sort of intensive critiquing can be helpful, but it can also be threatening, especially if writers have invested a great deal of themselves in the paper. To minimize anxiety and keep the critiques balanced and productive, we often play a variation of Peter Elbow's believing and doubting game ("Methodological Doubting and Believing: Contraries in Inquiry" in *Embracing Contraries: Explorations in Learning and Teaching*, New York: Oxford University Press, 1986, 254-300). If one group member suggests that a particular point could be moved to a different spot in the paper, another will defend the present location, or vice versa, with the writer listening quietly and remembering who the paper really belongs to. Also, many helpful responses do not need to imply positive or negative judgments. Group members can wonder aloud why the writer has chosen one word over another. They might want to hear about a particular incident in more detail. Or they can simply summarize what they perceive to be main points. Such nonjudgmental summaries, especially if written out and given to the writer, can be most useful in revealing how well the writer's overall intentions have come across to others.

> This sort of intensive critiquing can be helpful, but it can also be threatening, especially if writers have invested a great deal of themselves in the paper.

Wrapping it Up

While all of these stages tend to overlap and blur into each other, this is especially true as the end comes into view. I get the class to produce as many drafts as possible, but am also aware of deadlines and the need to move on to another project. Most projects take about two to three weeks to complete. Often, as we near the end, I begin to hear grumblings of discontent. "I'm getting really tired of this," one student might say. "I think I'm starting to make it *worse* instead of *better*," another might add. Group discussions may start to wander onto current ski conditions or whether next semester's course schedule is out yet. If so, it is time to wrap the project up, time to polish the style, edit for tense shifts and dangling modifiers, check format and documentation, make final revisions of the opening and closing paragraphs, proofread, and turn in the finished papers.

> . . . it is time to wrap the project up, time to polish the style, edit for tense shifts and dangling modifiers, check format and documentation, make final revisions of the opening and closing paragraphs, proofread, and turn in the finished papers.

I like to make some ceremony of completing a project. Usually students pass the finished papers around their group to share before finally turning them in. They've become so involved with one another's work that they want to see the end result. After collecting the papers, I read some aloud so class members can hear what was going on in groups other than their own. I may talk about how I think the project went, and I usually ask students to tell me what they found especially difficult or helpful. Then, if there is time left, I may have them free write about the project, or just let them go early, telling them we'll get started on a new project next time.

In closing, I'd like to emphasize two points. First, the overall flow of activities that I've been describing is not a rigid, lock-step process. In practice, the individual composing styles of my students vary widely, and for this reason activities that prove highly useful to one student may not be especially productive for another. In order to identify and accommodate these individual differences, I often make a conference sign-up list and encourage students who want individual attention to pop out of their discussion groups for five or ten-minute conferences while class is in session.

Second, the overall flow of activities described here can easily be modified depending on the class level, the needs and interests of the students, and the overall objectives of the writing project. For instance, projects involving the personal essay would have a different flow from projects emphasizing research or argumentation. Projects in a freshman class would not be as complex as those in an advanced class. Sometimes I have students specify their audience early in the writing process. Other times I wait until they are further along.

> . . . the overall flow of activities described here can easily be modified depending upon the class level, the needs and interests of the students, and the overall objectives of the writing project.

Despite these variations, however, the sequencing of activities is not random or capricious. The goal is to provide a structured learning environment that emphasizes writing as discovery and communication, not simply recording and arranging, to create a flow of learning activities that offer support and guidance throughout the writing process.

The Roots of Organic Form in Poetry

It is becoming clear that organic form, or free verse, is neither a temporary phenomenon nor a sudden rejection of established tradition, but a natural evolution of that tradition, an attempt to get beyond the inherent limitations of static, mechanical form and reaffirm natural speech rhythms as the foundation of poetry.

Of course, we can never go back, never ignore developments of the past few hundred years. It would be naïve to try, but in an increasingly mechanized and depersonalized post-industrial society, we should not be surprised to find poets reasserting a vision of creative expression that does not force people to become mere functionaries, subordinating the call of the muse to formal conventions. In a sense, then, this process resembles simultaneous trends in the other arts: primitivism and expressivism in the visual arts; or the inclusion of dissonance and folk themes in music, whether by Ralph Vaughan Williams, Aaron Copland, George Gershwin, or Miles Davis.

> Such breaks with tradition may be seen as bold departures, but they spring from existing roots.

Such breaks with formal tradition may be bold departures, but they spring from existing roots. It is interesting here to compare Gerard Manley Hopkins and Walt Whitman, the first drawing much of his poetic strength from his passionate struggle for liberation, and the second sounding his "barbaric yawp" in joyous defiance of accepted conventions—both men, though of vastly different temperaments, natural descendants of the romantics in their yearnings for self-expression and freedom, the two of them learning to say in the *form* of their poetry what Shelley and Byron had been saying in the *content* of theirs.

The fundamental liberties granted by free verse, however, have been technical rather than spiritual or political. No longer tied to rigid stanzaic patterns, the poem can go literally any way the poet wants. It can be any length or width, with regular, irregular, or "kind of regular" stanzas. Lines can be broken into breath units, thought units, image clusters, or just whenever the poet wants. Rhyme can be keyed into syntactical structures, used randomly, hinted at through alliteration and assonance, or strictly avoided.

Unfortunately, this proliferation of technical experimentation has not been matched by a comparable development of our critical tools, leaving us the sad situation in which the prosody of much of our best recent poetry cannot be discussed except in terms that are either very general or of very limited currency. We seem to be waiting nostalgically for a return to the fixed forms rather than making a serious effort to come to terms with open forms. As a result, the embarrassing fact remains that 155 years after the publication of the 1855 edition of *Leaves of Grass*, at a time when most serious poetry is being written in open forms, we have taken only a few small steps toward developing the kind of consistent and comprehensive poetic theory that we can rely on iwhen discussing the fixed forms. Perhaps when we have learned to stop viewing organic form as a temporary aberration in or an abandonment of our tradition of English language poetry and see it as a natural extension of that tradition, we will finally come to terms with it.

> We seem to be waiting nostalgically for a return to the fixed forms rather than making a serious effort to come to terms with open forms.

In order to go forward, however, we must first go backward and look briefly at the traditions from which free verse has grown, especially the classical syllable-counting prosodic patterns that came to dominate English poetry from about the time of Chaucer until the twentieth century. These patterns, grafted onto or superimposed over our much more fluid and free-flowing native alliterative and syllable-stress rhythms, were Greek in origin and were quantitative, based in that language, as in Latin, upon the relative length rather than the relative stress of syllables. These and the more recent Italian and French verse forms were deemed somehow more refined and elegant than anything a rude Anglo-Saxon heritage could hope to produce.

> These and the more recent Italian and French verse forms were deemed somehow more refined and elegant than anything a rude Anglo-Saxon heritage could hope to produce.

With the accelerated building of both classical and contemporary Continental influences from, say, the time of Chaucer's death (1400) until the death of Queen Elizabeth I (1603), native stress-based, alliterative verse forms became more and more thoroughly subordinated to these fixed, syllable-and-line counting forms. Gradually, from about the time of Donne until the twentieth century, however, native speech rhythms have begun to re-assert themselves until, increasingly frustrated by the limiting qualities of the fixed forms, poets today are finally breaking free to sing again in their native voices.

An examination of five sonnets written over this period shows how this movement back to natural speech rhythms occurred and how it relates to our exploration of the roots of organic form.

It is difficult today to look clearly at the poetry of Sir Thomas Wyatt. His poems can seem strained and artificial to modern readers, who place great value on spontaneity and naturalness. And yet along with this artificiality, the poems often have a beguiling quaintness, an innocence something like a fawn trying to take those first few faltering steps. We feel a certain lumpy crudeness, accentuated rather than hidden by the ornaments of style.

But for all of this, we understand that Wyatt is generally regarded as a premier craftsman, as the man who, in E. M. W. Tillyard's words, "let the Renaissance into English verse," rescuing it from a period when it had been floundering about for many years unable either to commit itself to emulating the Continental patterns that had flashed out so brilliantly in Chaucer or to retreat contentedly back into the more homely native tradition rooted in alliteration and stress patterns.

> While John Skelton allowed the two traditions about equal footing in his "Skeltonics," Wyatt took the crucial step of forcing native rhythms to submit to the syllable-and-line counting patterns again.

While John Skelton allowed the two traditions about equal footing in his "Skeltonics," Wyatt took the crucial step of forcing native rhythms to submit to the syllable-and-line counting patterns. Still, particularly in Wyatt's early work, the native influences are very evident, and as C.S. Lewis points out, are responsible for much of the poetry's real charm. In his translations from Petrarch, Sannazarro, and others, however, Wyatt is clearly scrambling and unsure of himself, almost totally lacking in that quintessential quality of the best Petrarchan poetry, *sprezzatura*, as is evident in his translation of the following sonnet from Sannazarro, which appears in Tottel's *Miscellany* as "The Lover's Life Compared to the Alps":

> *Like to these unmeasureable mountains*
> *Is my painful life the burden of ire;*
> *For of great height be they, and high is my desire:*
> *And I of tears, and they be full of fountains;*

Under craggy rocks they have full barren plains,
Hard thoughts in me my woeful mind doth tire;
Small fruit and many leaves their tops do attire.
Small effect with great trust in me remains.

The boisterous winds oft their high boughs do blast,
Hot sighs from me continually be shed;
Cattle in them, and in me love is fed;
Immovable am I, and they are full steadfast;
Of restless birds they have the tune and note,
And I always plaints that pass through my throat.

Wyatt is like a Kansas aristocrat driving down Main Street in the bright new Maserati he brought back from a Cook's Tour of Italy. He smiles condescendingly at the local peasants, maybe waves and shouts *ciao* to a few of the more fortunate ladies, who can't help turning their heads. They are impressed. He is cultured. Sophisticated. Nobody notices the manure on his boots. That, in Kansas, is the norm. What gets noticed is the Continental flair that sets him apart and causes others to try to imitate him.

Yet seen from this distance in time, the degree to which Wyatt has failed to integrate the Continental style with his native tradition may well seem the most important quality of his work. The burden of his ire, we feel, couldn't possibly be more painful than the ponderous rhythmic pattern of the first two lines, between which the only enjambment of the poem occurs. After this we get a long chain of conceits in which the syntactical units and natural speech rhythms are rudely forced to accommodate themselves to the demands of the set form, yet do not do so. Lines leap out, almost as exasperated comments on the whole process of making the poem: "Under craggy rocks they have full barren plains" might be considered an apt description of Wyatt's technique with the iambic pentameter line. "Hard thoughts in me my woeful mind doth tire" is as thoroughly convincing in its context as is "Small effect with great trust in me remains" two lines later when we find that he intends to carry the poem through to the end whatever the cost. Carry it through he does, though, and not too badly when his position in history is considered, for despite its stumbling awkwardness, this, along with his other sonnets, succeeded in establishing the convention in English. It's as though Wyatt's message to English poetry was—It isn't easy, folks, but by God, it *can* be done.

> It's as though Wyatt's message to English poetry was—It isn't easy, folks, but by God, it *can* be done.

For all his importance to our literary tradition, however, Wyatt never got beyond a rather crude and awkward handling of the European conventions. It was for later writers, building largely on his example, to master the sonnet, learning how to extend and focus a metaphor, how to join opposites into a conceit that would seem at once absurd and perfectly appropriate, how to modulate natural speech rhythms with alliteration and assonance so that sound and sense would flow more smoothly into the iambic pentameter framework, how to build currents of rhetorical energy that would push readers around line endings, de-emphasizing the impact of a rhyme before cutting the current off at the end of a quatrain, or bringing the reader down hard on a crucial rhyme, giving a sense of finality and completion.

Nor did it take long for this to happen. Shakespeare's "Sonnet 73," for example, shows such complete mastery of sonnet conventions that it seems to shimmer towards us from another language than Wyatt's. It combines the perfect balance and finely chiseled elegance of classical Greece with the smooth-flowing golden timbre of the Italian Renaissance. And yet it is thoroughly and completely English. Its structure is probably as artificial and consciously contrived as that of any poem in our language, yet when has a poem ever felt more natural, more plainly spoken, more sincere?

> *That time of year thou mayst in me behold*
> *When yellow leaves, or none, or few do hang*
> *Upon those boughs which shake against the cold,*
> *Bare ruined choirs where late the sweet birds sang.*
> *In me thou seest the twilight of such day*
> *As after sunset fadeth in the west,*
> *Which by and by black night doth take away*
> *Death's second self that seals up all in rest.*
> *In me thou seest the glowing of such fire*
> *That on the ashes of his youth does lie,*
> *As on the deathbed whereon it must expire,*
> *Consumed with that which it was nourished by.*
> > *This thou perceiv'st which makes thy love more strong.*
> > *To love that well, which thou must leave ere long.*

Here is the complete assurance of the master in total command of his powers, from the subtly modulated harmonics of line one to the trembling ambiguity of "well" in line 14. So effortless. Just something he tossed off between plays.

> So effortless. Just something he tossed off between plays.

And yet it all falls together, building in intensity and power right up to the final couplet, where all the implications of the first 12 lines focus on the two words, "This thou," which vibrate back up through the poem sonically as well as conceptually.

The poem's music is organized on the familiar (thanks to C.S. Lewis) pattern of theme and variations, the variations preceding and gradually honing in on the theme upon which they are based, and finally identifying it in the concluding couplet. What draws us forward into the poem, then, is largely its arrangement—the fact that its source, the focal point of its energy, comes at the end, which pulls the reader toward it like a magnet. Each quatrain gently probes an image, building it into a metaphor, exploring and extending it with appeals to the reader's sight, hearing, reason, and emotion, yet amidst the wealth of images, the issues are fundamental, defined by primal opposites, warmth and cold, light and darkness, life and death. The theme emerges slowly, however, as the poem's time frame narrows from the cycle of a year, to a day about to fade, where the first note of death is sounded, to the very instant of expiration of the last coal of a once brilliantly glowing fire. And then the couplet pulls it all together. If there is music in poetry, surely it is here.

The first quatrain, built upon that well-worn metaphor about the autumn of life, avoids triteness by making autumn visual, unfolding it in an image that is extended and explored through three lines. Then in line four, as the boughs are compared to the choirs of a ruined cathedral, a second metaphor extends out of the vehicle of the first, not mixed but carefully calculated to enrich and intensify the first before all the accumulated force of both metaphors is brought to bear upon "sang."

> If there is music in poetry, surely it is here.

Meanwhile certain things have been happening to our ears, our inner ears, the ones in our minds. These things are worth taking note of. The *l, th, w,* and *m* sounds, which will become so important in the couplet, are introduced in a beautiful texture of alliteration and assonance that would shame the gaudiness of the end rhymes, were they not so perfect, so brilliantly essential to the poem's total effect. Here, if anywhere, ornamentation and structure are one. The strange triad "yellow, none, or few" in line two comes down on "hang," leaving the reader hanging onto the sound while reaching back across to the start of line three for "upon." And the rhythm just goes on, specifying, focusing energy on "cold," then in line four, moving from the "bare, choirs, where" combination into "late the sweet" before returning to the *br* combination and finally yielding up "sang," the rhyme we have been waiting for since the end of line two. Perhaps now that the anticipatory pressure has been released, we can appreciate the implications of ambiguity in "late." For Shakespeare, the fixed form is clearly not an obstacle to expression; it is a means of expression. He has made the form his own.

> For Shakespeare, the fixed form is clearly not an obstacle to expression; it is a means of expression.

Donne's "Holy Sonnet 7," perhaps even more sophisticated than Shakespeare's poem, makes a different kind of music. After Shakespeare, English poets were forced either to go to the Italian form or show up as second rate. Donne, however, retains the concluding couplet and thus produces a kind of hybrid of the English and Italian styles. In some ways, his rough handling of the form would seem a step backward toward Wyatt rather than an advance in technical accomplishment. As in Wyatt, the dynamic, rhetorical energy of the speaker's voice making meaning struggles against the restraints of the static form. The voice of the octave blares like a powerful trumpet blast, surging around the ends of lines, furiously knocking aside any obstacle, leaving a wake of tangled corpses awash in untidy rhymes:

> At the round earth's imagined corners, blow
> Your trumpets, angels, and arise, arise
> From death, you numberless infinities
> Of soules, and to your scattered bodies go:
> All whom the flood did, and fire shall o'erthrow,
> All whom war, dearth, age, agues, tyrannies,
> Despair, law, chance, hath slain, and you whose eyes,

Shall behold God, and never taste death's woe.
But let them sleep, Lord, and me mourn a space,
For, if above all these, my sins abound,
'Tis late to ask abundance of thy grace,
When we are there; here on this lowly ground,
Teach me how to repent; for that's as good
As if thou hadst sealed my pardon with thy blood.

The urgent voice insists that what demands to be said is so compelling that the speaker can't be expected to fuss about details of "craft." The iambic meter is wrenched hard, almost beyond recognition in a few places. In such blind urgency, a half rhyme, if not quite as nice as a whole, will just have to do. Paradoxically, however, a closer look reveals that this is indeed a meticulous poem, that the apparently chaotic or sloppy quality is a precisely calculated device, another reminder—as though we needed it—of Donne's intellectual subtlety, his technical mastery.

By subverting the regularity of the prosodic pattern, Donne manages to free his subjective rhetorical voice from objective mechanical restraints, once again putting native English speech rhythms on an equal footing with the fixed mathematical form. In short, he breaks the rules, but he does so in such a carefully calculated way that he seems to be playing with the form rather than struggling against it, as Wyatt so clearly was. Donne, although he may pretend otherwise, is always in complete control. The imperfect rhyme of lines two and three, for instance, is mirrored in lines six and seven—but, even here, where we have been waiting for a perfect rhyme since line two, he gives us "arise" / "eyes," a rhyme to the ears, but not to the eyes. Accidental? We might think so, were it not for the "blow" / "go," "o'erthrow" / "woe" rhymes, where he does the same thing. Further subversion of conventional regularity occurs in the pairing off of "infinities" in line three with "bodies," which straddles the fourth and fifth feet of line four and competes with "go" as a potential rhyme word. Probably more striking than any of these carefully controlled irregularities, however, is the internal patterning of "earth's" / "death," "dearth" / "death's"—a combination that further undercuts the regularity of the fixed framework.

> It registers the dynamic sense of something being worked through, a vision coming into being, a problem being wrestled with, a resolution achieved.

Such loosening, even subverting, of the frame allows Donne to give his Senecan prose style more freedom to develop its own currents of rhythm, tone color, and meaning, freeing the subjective imperative from submission to external constraints of the convention. The rhetorical flow of words and ideas moves with the current of the poet's pulse. It registers the dynamic sense of something being worked through, a vision coming into being, a problem being wrestled with, a resolution achieved.

This ability to capture the personal contours of an idea was considered a principal virtue of the Senecan amble. Ideas were expected to work themselves out naturally, according to their own dynamic natures rather than be "licked into shape" in the Ciceronian fashion, which stressed balance, symmetry, and melodiousness as the essential qualities of a fine prose style. The Senecan style was more natural, more organic, more concerned with substance than with stylistic niceties. A sense of wildness and irregularity, even among practitioners of the terse style, was considered an asset. Keeping this in mind, we realize that Donne's prose rhythms are largely responsible for the restless, urgent, probing rhythm of the octave. After the initial introductory clause, "blow" establishes the imperative voice, and from that point the emotional energy explodes outward through the next seven lines. Phrase issues forth from phrase, image from image, catalogue from catalogue. Parallel structures are established, broken down, returned to, and broken down again. The result is a voice as turbulent and chaotic as the vision it embodies.

The abrupt shifting of gears, the slowing of tempo and quieting of voice that occurs in the first line of the sestet, results from the speaker's sudden recognition that his emotion has outstripped his reason, that he bears a heavy burden of personal sin and is therefore not ready for the final judgment. He sees further that it is precisely his wildness, his inability to properly control his passions, that causes his sinful condition.

He needs to repent. He moves slowly now. Deliberately. The rhymes are perfect. The pace is measured and even, dutifully compliant with the demands of the prosodic frame. Still, the frequent metrical inversions and substitutions remind us how difficult it is to tame that powerful nature— to make it bow to the Divine Will. "Teach me how to repent," he pleads. He wants to repent but doesn't know how. He can neither entirely tame his passionate nature nor finally even be sorry of it. He wishes he could repent, but some inner law of his being prevents him from doing so. This is the reason that his pardon has not necessarily been sealed by the blood of Christ. There, Donne knows, is the Teacher and the lesson. But the lesson remains unabsorbed on the visceral level.

Here is a poem of such subtlety, sophistication, and daring that more than 400 years after its composition many serious readers of poetry may not appreciate its technical brilliance. It is easier to hear Shakespeare's music than Donne's because most of us have been taught to associate music in poetry with the regular patterning of sound that results from the presence of a fixed prosodic frame. Shakespeare gives great prominence to this form, exploiting its full range of possibilities while simultaneously yielding willingly to its demands. This allows us to experience his sonnet as rhythmic, harmonic, and well proportioned. The personal voice of the poem is perfectly in accord with the regular structure of the frame, embellishing it, coloring it, charging it with implication and meaning. In Donne, however, the voice establishes a rhythm of its own, which competes for dominance with the quantitative music established by the form.

The resulting roughness, or irregularity, produces an impression of dissonance and disorder, of something unbalanced and turbulent. This does not, however, mean that the poem is "unmusical." Surely, dissonance, asymmetry, and roughness are vital characteristics of much of our greatest music. Nor does the turbulence indicate a failure of craft, as the term "unmusical" sometimes implies. On the contrary, the roughness is a precisely calculated effect, brilliantly executed. Instead of keying his speech rhythm *into* the quantitative pattern, Donne works it *against* the pattern so that the two melodic lines can run simultaneously *punctus contra punctum*, point against point—counterpoint.

> Instead of keying his speech rhythm *into* the quantitative pattern, Donne works it *against* the pattern so that the two melodic lines can run simultaneously *punctus contra punctum*, point against point—counterpoint.

Gerard Manley Hopkins' "Carrion Comfort" goes even further in asserting the dominance of dynamic personal

expression over static objective constraints. As in many of
his other sonnets, especially "Felix Randall" and "Spelt from
Sibyl's Leaves," the celebrated sprung rhythm combines with
the dense harmonic texture to bend the sonnet framework
almost beyond recognition—almost, but not quite:

> *Not, I'll not, carrion comfort, Despair, not feast on thee*
> *Not untwist—slack they may be—these last strands of man*
> *In me or, most weary, cry I can no more. I can;*
> *Can something, hope, wish day come, not choose not to be.*
> *But ah, but O thou terrible, why wouldst thou rude on me*
> *Thy wring-world right foot rock? lay a lionlimb against me? scan*
> *With darksome devouring eyes my bruised bones? and fan*
> *O in turns of tempest, me heaped there; me frantic to avoid thee*
>   *and flee?*
> *Why? That my chaff might fly; my grain lie, sheer and clear*
> *Nay in all that toil, that coil, since (seems) I kissed the rod,*
> *Hand rather, my heart lo! lapped strength, stole joy, would*
>   *laugh, cheer.*
> *Cheer whom though? the hero whose heaven-handling flung me,*
>   *foot trod*
> *Me? or me that fought him? O which one? is it each one? That*
>   *night, that year*
> *Of now done darkness I wretch lay wrestling with (my God!)*
>   *my God.*

It may, as in line eight, take 18 syllables of twisting through
intricate arrangements of alliteration and assonance, past
more than one perfectly adequate rhyme word before Hopkins
ends a line, but he keeps the poem to 14 lines and observes
the traditional Italian rhyme scheme. In this, he is more
conventional than Donne, just as in maintaining the clean
break between octave and sestet he is more conventional than
Milton and Wordsworth often are.

Clearly, though, Hopkins has pushed the fixed form to the
breaking point. This is due to two factors: the poem is writ-

ten in six-stress sprung rhythm, and its harmonics are keyed primarily into dynamic syntactical and associational patterns rather than into a fixed, quantitative form.

Sprung rhythm, according to Hopkins' famous "Preface," is "the most natural of things." He goes on to specify that it is "the rhythm of common speech and of written prose, when rhythm is perceived in them" and to say further that it is an evolution from, or a stepping beyond, "Counterpoint Rhythm," which he finds in the choruses in Milton's *Samson Agonistes*, "but with the disadvantage that he [Milton] does not let the reader clearly know what the ground rhythm is meant to be, and so they have struck most readers as merely irregular." When the counter rhythm actually overcomes the primary rhythm, Hopkins says, "what is written is one rhythm only and probably Sprung Rhythm, of which I now speak." As such, sprung rhythm is both a step forward and a step backward. It is a springing beyond the mathematically based rhythms, and yet it is a return to the more fluid and varied rhythmic dynamics of "common speech and of written prose."

> The result is that while the sonnet frame remains, the poem seems to have sprung beyond it into something very much like free verse.

This shift in the rhythmic foundation of his verse was accompanied by another crucial but seldom remarked breakthrough: the focusing of alliteration, assonance, and internal rhyme upon the phrase and clause rather than upon the foot and line. The result is that, while the sonnet frame remains, the poem seems to have sprung beyond it into something very much like free verse. This becomes apparent as soon as we see what the poem might look like if the lines were broken differently:

Not, I'll not, carrion comfort, Despair,
Not feast on thee,
Not untwist—slack they may be—
These last strands of man in me
Or, most weary, cry I can
No more. I can, can something, hope
Wish day come, not choose not to be.
But ah, but O thou terrible, why
Wouldst thou rude
On me thy wring-world right foot
Rock? Lay a lionlimb against me? Scan
With darksome devouring eyes
My bruised bones? And fan,
O in turns of tempest, me
heaped there; me
Frantic to avoid thee and flee?

Few, given the poem in this form, could reconstruct it into something that would pass for a sonnet.

Why? That my chaff might fly;
My grain lie, sheer and clear. Nay in all that toil,
That coil, since (seems) I kissed the rod, hand rather,
My heart lo! lapped strength, stole joy,
Would laugh, cheer. Cheer whom though?
The hero whose heaven-handling
Flung me, foot trod me? Or me
That fought him? O which one? is it each one?
That night, that year of now done darkness
I wretch lay wrestling with (my God!) my God.

Few, given the poem in this form, could reconstruct it into something that would pass for a sonnet. All that remains of the prosodic frame now is the division between octave and sestet and the 14 rhyme words, which are still six stresses apart. But who could locate these stresses with certainty, or distinguish the end rhymes from the internal ones?

When arranged this way on the page, the poem's dependence on prose rhythms becomes clear. The rhythm, which is essentially dynamic, is controlled by the speaker's subjective imperative—the desperate searching for a reason to live, for release from anguish, from fear. The octave's dominant rhetorical movement is from an attitude of forced courage, through a gradual erosion of this resolve, into an avalanche of frighteningly destructive questions, each focused with a distinct alliterative signature: first a *w-r* pattern, next *l-m*, then a *d-b* pattern, and finally a matrix of *f-t-h*. At the same time, the long *e* sound, prominent all through the octave, emerges into complete dominance, driving home the fundamental issue: "me" "thee" "flee." The movement of the sestet is similar to that of the octave, so much so that it seems almost an echo. Once again the tentative note of certainty is established, apparently sweeping away the ominous questioning of the octave with an answer that proceeds from a higher level of understanding, but this too crumples. Cheer the one who tortures me? Cheer myself for fighting him? Who is it tortures me? Satan? God? I, myself? Or all three? The pace is fast and powerful—each question growing out of a previous one, moving relentlessly forward to the final explosion of astonished recognition at the end. Here again, also, the harmonics are clearly keyed into the pulse of the rhetorical current. If this poem is mathematically regular in some significant ways, those ways are, nevertheless, pretty variable.

> The pace is fast and powerful—each question growing out of a previous one, moving relentlessly forward to the final explosion of astonished recognition at the end.

Perhaps the best argument for calling it a sonnet is that Hopkins considered it to be one. That is, while writing it, he had a definite plan in mind. He knew how many lines it would be, where the lines would break, how often he would have to repeat a rhyme. He also understood that his poem would have two major divisions—one of eight lines, the other of six—and that the second would offer an answer or reply to the first. While admittedly pretty general, this kind of knowledge is important in that it gives the poet a sense of going to a known destination by a familiar route. He has a sense of the scope and range of the form. At any point he knows how far along he is in the process of writing. And he knows when he is done. In a very real sense, then, the verse is not free. It is still bound, however loosely, to a fixed prosodic frame, the net of Frost's often quoted tennis simile: "Writing free verse is like playing tennis without a net."

And yet a fixed pattern was as often an ally as an obstacle to poetic expression. It allowed the poet to be pulled along by the demands of the form, working out necessary arrangements of sound and meaning so as to arrive on time with a perfect rhyme. This need to "make a rhyme" combined with the need to extend or tie off a thought actually helps solve many problems of progression and closure.

Once the pattern is set aside, however, poets are left with nothing but the sound of their own voice making meaning to guide them along. The poem becomes an organic expression of the poet's thoughts and feelings flowing into language, projecting itself forward into silence, as in the conclusion of "The Leaden Echo and the Golden Echo":

> Oh then, weary then why should we tread? O why are we so
> 	haggard at the heart, so care-coiled, care-killed, so fagged,
> 	so fashed, so cogged, so cumbered,
> When the thing we fondly forfeit is kept with fonder a care,
> Far with fonder a care (and we, we should have lost it) finer,
> 	fonder
> A care kept.—Where kept? Do but tell us where kept, where.

Yonder.—What high as that! We follow, now we follow.
    Yonder, yes yonder, yonder,
Yonder.

Of this poem, Hopkins said, "I have marked the stronger stresses, but with the degree of stress so perpetually varying no marking is satisfactory. Do you think all had best be left to the reader?" To which we might reply, Why not? It's free verse isn't it?

Teaching Creative Writing: A Review Essay

Creative Writing in America: Theory and Pedagogy, edited by Joseph M. Moxley (Urbana, IL: N.C.T.E., 1989, 272 pages).

Released into Language, Wendy Bishop (Urbana, IL: N.C.T.E., 1990, 233 pages).

Writing Poems, 3rd ed., Robert Wallace (New York: Harper Collins, 1991, 458 pages).

What If? Writing Exercises for Fiction Writers, Anne Bernays and Pamela Painter (New York: Harper Collins, 1990, 230 pages).

The College Handbook of Creative Writing, Robert DeMaria (New York: Harcourt Brace Jovanovich, 1991, 359 pages).

Taken together, these five books offer an illuminating overview of current issues and practices in teaching creative writing. They portray a highly evolved writing tradition in search of identity as an academic discipline, a situation with which many compositionists will be familiar. For just as composition can trace its roots back to classical rhetoric, creative writing can point to a proud tradition extending back to Homer, and beyond. In spite of such ancient heritage, however, creative writing, like composition, is in the process of redefining and reasserting itself within the academy. Such a process necessarily involves an attempt to identify and define the central paradigmatic features of the field. While compositionists have taken this task up eagerly, creative writers have not been so quick to do so. Among these books, Joseph Moxley's *Creative Writing in America: Theory and Pedagogy*, offers the most comprehensive overview of creative writing instruction. This anthology is divided into four sections that cover fundamental assumptions, the creative process, editing and publishing, and goals and methods. As Moxley says in his Preface:

> *At present, no debate rages in professional journals as to whether creative writing programs are providing students with the necessary writing skills, knowledge of the composing process, or background in literature to write well. . . . Yet there is evidence that our discipline is preparing to undergo a paradigm shift, a period of self-reflexiveness in which we question our theories and practices. (xi)*

This theme is taken up by all four essays in the first section, but most notably by George Garrett and Eve Shelnutt.

> Garrett sees this tradition taking hold in America in the form of "great books" courses and composition courses "that permitted or, indeed, required the students to write poems or stories."

In "The Future of Creative Writing Programs," before projecting a future, George Garrett looks back to determine how creative writing programs have evolved to their present state. Interestingly, he traces creative writing's roots to "the composition of original Latin poetry and prose" during the Renaissance and portrays current trends as "a *renewal, a revival*, the return, in somewhat different form and circumstances, of an old-fashioned, centuries-old form of teaching and learning rhetoric" (48). He sees this tradition taking hold in America in the form of "great books" courses and composition courses "that permitted or, indeed, required the students to write poems or stories" (48). This tradition was gradually extended and formalized through the participation of creative writers on college faculties, the inception of the Iowa Writers' Workshop in 1937, and the founding of Associated Writing Programs "in the middle of the 1960's" by R. V. Cassill (55). Given this historical perspective, Garrett argues for a future that locates creative writing as a unifying center of literary and rhetorical studies:

> . . . *for at a time when reading and writing are a serious problem and a great cultural illiteracy prevails, creative writing is one antidote to toxic ignorance, all the more effective because it is somewhat disguised and different from humdrum composition courses. Students are still learning rhetoric and the habits of close reading and careful writing in creative writing courses. (56)*

After taking some initial umbrage at Garrett's characterization of composition courses as "humdrum," I can see that he is speaking of an impoverished skill-and-drill mentality, not of more recent efforts to reconnect composition to its rhetorical heritage. Similarly, the reference to "cultural illiteracy," which initially calls to mind E. D. Hirsch and Harold Bloom, appears in the context of the whole essay to speak to a larger concern for enlarging human understanding through reading and writing. As Garrett says:

> Eve Shelnutt argues that creative writing has been severed from its intellectual roots.

> *If we are training young writers to write well, competently, without also teaching them how to recognize and value excellence for its own sake, substantial as well as technical excellence, we are wasting their time and ours. (59)*

Many of Garrett's concerns are shared by Eve Shelnutt. Her essay, "Notes From a Cell: Creative Writing Programs in Isolation," argues that creative writing has been severed from its intellectual roots:

*Critics of the more than 280 graduate and undergraduate
writing programs in colleges and universities across the
country would no doubt answer that they never expected
"real" writers to emerge from the cocoon of academe, much less
intellectuals from among those writers. (3)*

She is especially concerned about the proliferation of
M.F.A. programs and the "Brat Pack" they are producing.
Believing that most M.F.A. programs are driven primarily by
a concern to produce marketable writers, she sees the recent
propagation of literary journals as an
attempt to augment publication outlets
and credentials for graduates. Similarly,
she believes that most writing studied
by M.F.A. candidates is read with an eye
toward spotting trends and watching
the competition rather than with
serious consideration of the literary
substance of the work. Meanwhile, not only are these students
isolated from the central intellectual currents of literature,
they are also largely ignorant of recent developments in
composition, even though they usually subsidize their educa-
tions (and may support themselves after graduation) by
teaching in that area.

> She is especially
> concerned about
> the proliferation
> of M.F.A. programs
> and the "Brat Pack"
> they are producing.

While recognizing the difficulties inherent in teaching
imaginative writing in an intellectual climate that is itself
unstable, Shelnutt returns again to the central theme of
isolation:

*But if M.F.A. students and their faculty knit themselves into
tight cocoons of unexamined curricula, of defensive responses
to literature and composition programs, and of provincial views
of success in the field of writing, how are they to participate
not only in a worldwide community of writers, but also in a
global community of thinkers? (19)*

These are serious questions indeed, and while the very asking might seem at first glance to throw the whole enterprise of creative writing instruction into serious doubt, a second thought suggests that these are precisely the kinds of hard questions that must be asked if this time-honored writing tradition is to find a worthy place in contemporary American academia.

If other sections of the book are less noteworthy than the first, they are often interesting. Three essays that stand out for me personally are Robert H. Abel's "One Writer's Apprenticeship," Donald M. Murray's "Unlearning to Write," and Valerie Miner's "The Book in the World." These and several others often approach their subjects from fresh perspectives, focusing on how to link the classroom with the world of publishing, for instance, or on the similarities and differences between expository and imaginative writing.

This possible connectedness between composition and creative writing is also a striking feature of Wendy Bishop's *Released into Language*. Indeed, the book draws heavily upon composition research for both its theoretical foundation and its practical applications. Bishop clearly sees "writing" as a unified field and moves freely among references to Sharon Crowley, John Berryman, Nancy Sommers, F. Scott Fitzgerald, Mina Shaughnessy, and Anne Sexton without much regard to whether their work is traditionally associated with composition or creative writing. In doing so, she identifies herself most closely with the theories of James Britton. After a brief discussion of expressive, transactional, and poetic discourse, she explains that "Britton and his colleagues' discourse taxonomy helps me to understand the division of writing labor as it now exists in English Departments, and why, somewhat backwardly, we divide writing instruction by types of written products" (29).

Bishop favors a more holistic approach centered in exploration (expressive discourse) and evolving toward instrumental (transactional) or imaginative (poetic) discourse as the writer's ideas and purposes are clarified in the act of writing.

> Much of the writing is generated in class through a variety of activities and exercises drawn from both composition and creative writing sources.

To foster this approach and to maintain her emphasis on writing as *process*, Bishop favors a workshop course format, yet one that differs from the more traditional creative writing workshop with its heavy emphasis upon critique and revision. Bishop's workshop, which she calls the "transactional creative writing workshop," encompasses all stages of the writing process and includes a variety of activities ranging from the standard "full-group critique" to "performance," "student-led discussion," and "one-to-one conferencing— student to teacher *and* peer to peer" (44). Much of the writing is generated in class through a variety of activities and exercises drawn from both composition and creative writing sources. In her chapter "Ten Inventions and Variations," she offers selected assignments, complete with suggestions for their use and examples of completed work by her students and herself. She advocates the teacher's doing an assignment whenever possible to get a feel for its levels of opportunity and difficulty. As in many creative writing courses, students submit a portfolio of finished work, which is considered along with other factors in determining the final course grade. Chapter Eight, "Evaluating and Responding," contains sample critique sheets for mid-semester and final evaluations. "Appendix A" is a series of "Response Protocol Sheets" for in-class use, and "Appendix B" is "A Selected, Annotated Bibliography" on teaching creative writing.

Wendy Bishop has clearly done an outstanding job of integrating her vast research and experience into an innovative and effective teaching package. For this, she deserves high praise and many readers. Certainly most of those readers, whether in composition or creative writing, will come away with enlarged awareness and practical ideas to improve their teaching. If pressed to say something negative, I might refuse. Or I might confess that finally I find it just a bit *too* systematic, too reliant on method and technique, without enough acknowledgment of or allowance for the messy and mysterious, the sublime and grotesque. For instance, in Chapter Two we have references to Anne Sexton, Robert Lowell, and John Berryman; but students are seldom challenged, as readers or writers, to come to terms with the kinds of crucial issues that these poets dealt with, focusing instead on metaphors for writing or on the creative use of cliché. As Bishop points out, quoting Jim Heynan, poetry involves both craft and vision (40). The philosophy and pedagogy elaborated here are very strong on craft, but somewhat less so on vision.

> Wendy Bishop has clearly done an outstanding job of integrating her vast research and experience into an innovative and effective teaching package.

In *Writing Poems*, Robert Wallace deals with this issue explicitly in Chapter Eight, "Beyond the Rational: Burglars and Housedogs," but he speaks to it implicitly throughout, partly with outstanding examples of student and non-student (I hesitate to say "professional") poets ranging from Sir Philip Sidney through Jorie Graham, and partly with unwavering respect for the mystery of it all: "The poet's technical experience, technical readiness, is like a finely tuned radio apparatus that is activated by the message, whenever it comes" (284).

Wallace might even agree with David St. John: "I cannot emphasize enough the importance of making young writers read. Beginning writers have neither the reading experience nor the writing experience to offer much more than the most trite poems about the most conventional subjects" (Moxley 189). More likely, Wallace knows that the "Great Models" and the "Sure-fire Exercise" approaches are the Scylla and Charybdis of creative writing instruction. Throughout this book, Wallace most often steers toward the former, yet always avoids wreckage, somehow managing to follow a course of authenticity and understanding through the tangled currents of contemporary poetics.

> ...Wallace knows that the "Great Models" and the "Sure-fire Exercise" approaches are the Scylla and Charybdis of creative writing instruction.

Even so, the book does favor what might loosely be termed a deductive method. The twelve chapters, for instance, are gathered into three sections: "Form: The Necessary Nothing," "Content: The Essential Something," and "Process: Making the Poem Happen." While Wallace speaks of this organization as "primarily a convenience of exposition, not an implicit theory" and invites users "to skip around freely" (xiii), this pattern of moving from conceptualization to experimentation is fundamental to the book's approach. Just as the overall design encourages teachers and students to try "Making the Poem Happen" only after studying form and content, individual chapters tend to begin with definitions and claims, followed by examples and illustrations, followed by "Questions and Suggestions," a collection of questions and activities designed to show understanding and foster creative expression.

Chapter Nine, "Starting a Poem: Wind, Sail, and Rigging," offers an interesting illustration of how Wallace connects composing and understanding. He begins with a discussion of old and new, imitation and originality. In a short passage heavily laden with references to Waller, Chaucer, Yeats, Pound, Eliot, and Dryden, Wallace tells us, *Tradition* is the long handle that gives force to the blow of the new, sharp head of the axe" (280). Then, in a section called "Imitation, Masters, Models, and So Forth," he explores imitation and parody before finally arriving at "Stirrings," an extremely thoughtful discussion of the poetic impulse—how it may be nurtured, sustained, brought to fruition. The discussion is extended and elaborated with a detailed look at the composition of William Stafford's "Ask Me" and of Wallace's own composing strategies as he wrote "Swimmer in the Rain."

Next, he moves to a promising section called "Talking to Oneself," which bogs down in warnings about sentimentality and overstatement; then he refines that into a discussion of deliberate overstatement and understatement before concluding with a discussion of Donne's use of hyperbole in "The Sun Rising" (299, 300). Finally, a brief concluding section called "Tacking" brings back the chapter's central sailing metaphor and relates it to sustaining and developing the initial poetic impulse. After this, "Questions and Suggestions" offers a number of interesting writing suggestions, none relating to over- or understatement; and finally, "Poems to Consider" provides a mini-anthology of eight poems.

> Wallace tells us, "*Tradition* is the long handle that gives force to the blow of the new, sharp head of the axe."

The individual components of the book are all useful and well-presented, but the overall pedagogical strategy is hazy and underinformed. Why no mention of meditation or the unconscious? Why are discussions of free writing so limited? Why not more accounts of the struggles of student

> Wallace writes with grace and wit. His book offers a wealth of information, advice, and inspiration.

and professional writers bringing poems into being? Yet despite these reservations, this is a fine book—one I'd order in a minute for my own classes because of its warmth, intelligence, and contagious love of making poems. Wallace writes with grace and wit. His book offers a wealth of information, advice, and inspiration.

What If? Writing Exercises for Fiction Writers is similarly inspiring but takes a very different instructional approach, downplaying theory and technical terminology in favor of practical activities intended to get students writing at the outset. Like Wallace, Bernays and Painter advocate studying great writers: "Buy their books and read them; study specific passages, write in the margins, type out their sentences. Absorbing the work of great writers is the best education of all" (xix). As though to underline this, the book's final section, "Learning from the Greats," offers five lessons that show how professional authors can be used for inspiration and imitation. Unlike Wallace, however, Bernays and Painter seldom examine great works in detail to illustrate their own ideas. Instead, they present brief quotations without comment in the context of a writing exercise or as epigraph or postscript to a lesson.

This book favors doing and making over understanding and analyzing. The eighty-three lessons are collected into twelve sections, each centered on a dominant concern such as character or dialogue. Within a given section, individual lessons typically begin with a paragraph or two of introductory comment followed by subsections entitled "The Exercise," "The Objective," and "Student Example." While most lessons are original to the authors, several are borrowed, with appropriate acknowledgement, from other writers such as William Kittredge or Alison Lurie. Although Painter and Bernays never make explicit any overriding organizational theory, the lessons do progress according to a system, earlier exercises focusing on getting started and later ones on structure and technique.

One notable absence is any significant attention to revision. Despite the authors' observation that "first drafts are apt to be a mess—this holds true for even the most accomplished writers" (167), only one lesson, "Identifying Story Scenes During Revision," tackles the subject head on. More characteristically, exercises focus on generating and shaping fiction. They assume the need for future revision, but offer little guidance in how to go about it.

Thus, while the book is strong in its varied suggestions for discovering potential stories and for using fictional techniques to explore and develop that potential, a lack of emphasis on "finishing" stories gives the impression that most students would be left with a number of notebook entries and perhaps a few completed drafts but little if any work that received much sustained attention or was carried all the way through the writing process.

While most lessons are original to the authors, several are borrowed, with appropriate acknowledgement, from other writers such as William Kittredge or Alison Lurie.

Even so, the authors do provide a wealth of provocative, stimulating activities designed to help students get into the act of writing fiction. These range from practice beginning *in medias res* to a lesson called "Put Your Heart on the Page," which features a quote from William Kittredge, "If you are not *risking* sentimentality, you are not close to your inner self" (23). The objectives of these exercises are clearly spelled out, and student examples are generally provided (but not for "Put Your Heart on the Page"). In all, *What If?* offers an innovative, exploratory approach to teaching fiction writing. Fresh, engaging, and practical, it looks especially appealing for a beginning course.

> At the end of each chapter, a few exercises appear. Seldom does much thought appear to have been given to their effectiveness.

The College Handbook of Creative Writing by Robert DeMaria is a very different book, an apparent effort to carry the *Harbrace Handbook* method over from composition into creative writing. As though anticipating reservations to the very concept, DeMaria begins somewhat defensively:

This book does not aim to be prescriptive. It does not tell the student what to write or how to write it. Instead it describes how universal writing problems have been dealt with by experienced writers, and it explains how the mistakes commonly made by novice writers can be avoided. (v)

And so, with Zenlike accuracy, DeMaria hits the mark without aiming: he does not show students what to do or how to do it. Instead, he provides great models and suggestions for avoiding error.

At the end of each chapter, a few exercises appear. Seldom does much thought appear to have been given to their effectiveness. No examples of student performance are provided. A few typical exercises, drawn from various chapters, may indicate the amount of imagination and teaching experience that have gone into this aspect of the book:

—Write a short story that takes place in a foreign country that you have never been to. (44)

—Write a poem about some aspect of nature, using as many images as possible. (261)

—Visit the zoo and describe some of the animals. Rely on observation, not memory or stereotypes. (159)

But this is not a book about enabling writing. It is a book about extrinsic definitions, admonitions, and motivations:

"Suspense is a condition created by uncertainty" (74), "The period is commonly used to end a declarative sentence or even an imperative sentence" (293), "Avoid the vague use of the term *plot*" (66), "Marketing your writing is the next step" (319). The last paragraph of the last chapter of the book deals with the problem of taxes:

> *The net loss or gain on schedule C is subtracted from or added to one's adjusted gross income. There are, however, limitations on how many years a writer can claim a loss. (327)*

Yet if the book ends on a note of loss, it is reassuring to know that these losses can be deducted for a few years. And perhaps this is only realism, a way of consoling oneself for having invested so much in an enterprise that was doomed from the start to fail. I imagine a student, someone very much like me, asking: *Didn't my father warn me this could happen if I tried to become a writer? Can I deduct the price of this book? How can I deduct from an income of zero? Or—maybe I can get a job teaching Comp.*

And this all-too-familiar scenario again calls to mind the bond between composition and creative writing. Maybe the student I'm imagining will get that job teaching Comp, fend off starvation, placate father, read Wendy Bishop and Peter Elbow and James Britton, join (or start) a writing group, get access to a computer, take a course from Valerie Miner, design and publish and sell a book or journal, inspire others to do the same. Essays, poems, stories—people writing and reading and talking about that writing.

All five books reviewed here suggest to me that this may be starting to happen, that we are beginning to recognize and honor a fundamental connectedness between composition and creative writing—in our histories, in our goals, and in our methodologies.

Despite this connectedness, we also have our differences. No, composition and creative writing are not one thing. But as these five books make clear, our paths do intersect in interesting and significant ways. We all have much to learn from a dialogue on the subject, and we all have much to give.

Many Errors, a Little Rightness:
The Politics of Ezra Pound

"Many Errors, a little rightness," the phrase is Pound's. It comes from "Canto CXVI" and suggests that Pound himself was aware, toward the end, of the extent to which he had become ensnared in the web of his own errors and delusions.

In 1967 when Pound was 82 years old and living in Italy, he was visited by the poet Allen Ginsberg, who recently came to Pound's birthplace here in Hailey. At their meeting Pound told the younger poet, "The intention was bad—that's the trouble—anything I've done has been an accident—any good has been spoiled by my intentions— the preoccupation with stupid and irrelevant things." And a few minutes later, "but my worst mistake was the stupid suburban prejudice of anti-Semitism, all along, that spoiled everything" (Hyde 271).

> ". . . but my worst mistake was the stupid suburban prejudice of anti-Semitism, all along, that spoiled everything."

And yet, for all that error, which Pound himself acknowledged, in order to fully understand the man, we must also look at the rightness, that is to say, at the wholeness of the picture, and when we do, we may come to terms with, learn from, the paradoxes and contradictions that are so much a part of Ezra Pound and his work.

To do that, it helps to have a sense of context. Pound was born here in Hailey and perhaps retained some Idaho characteristics—a respect for hard work and plain-spoken bluntness—even after growing up in the East and spending most of his adulthood abroad.

A prodigious scholar and master of many languages, he was also a spiritual visionary. We sometimes hear it said of our Native American peoples that they believe the world is alive and sacred and holy, that we two-footed ones are brothers and sisters with the four-foots, and with the wings of the sky and the fishes of the sea. Pound, too, saw the world as sacred and enchanted. His religion might be called animist or pantheist or pagan. For him, the myths of Ancient Greece, the tales of Zeus and Hera, Ares and Aphrodite, Odysseus and Circe, were not just quaint stories but profoundly evocative imaginative pathways into the spirit world, much as tales of Coyote and Raven might be to a Native American.

He was disturbed by poverty and pollution and corporate greed—by the horrors of World War I and by the growing disparities between the upper and lower classes.

Yet Pound lived in a violent and terrifying time. Like many writers of the early twentieth century, he was cynical and disillusioned with the society he lived in. He was disturbed by poverty and pollution and corporate greed—by the horrors of World War I and by the growing disparities between the upper and lower classes. He helped his friend and fellow expatriate T.S. Eliot revise *The Wasteland*, and his own "Hugh Selwyn Maubelry" shows that he shared much of Eliot's unhappiness with the directions of modern society.

While Pound's friend "Possum" managed to find hope and solace in Anglo Catholicism, Pound attempted a more difficult and idiosyncratic synthesis of beliefs, creeds, and theories. If his spirituality was closely linked with the Paganism of ancient Greece, for a philosophy of personal conduct and political order, he looked to the East, to Confucianism where he found balance, continuity, harmony, respect for tradition.

Pound was also, and this more than anything may have been his undoing, interested in economics. He believed that many of the ills of modern European civilization were due to runaway capitalism, which he considered usurious, exploitative, destructive of true human and natural value, substituting cash values for spiritual ones, turning nature and humans into mere resources and consumers.

> He rejected the alternative of Marxism as too dogmatic, collectivist, and artistically repressive.

He rejected the alternative of Marxism as too dogmatic, collectivist, and artistically repressive. In his search for other answers, he ran upon the writings of Major C. H. Douglas and Silvio Gessell. Often referred to as "social credit theory," these ideas stressed that currency was a primary cause of economic ill health. Social creditors believed that the true wealth of a nation lay not in bullion or banknotes, both of which were of little intrinsic value, but in the natural bounty of a land and its people.

Money, social creditors claimed, was best seen as a tool for distributing and exchanging goods and services. The problem was that as currency began to take on a life of its own, it acted to constrict rather than aid distribution. In an idea much like Marx's theory of surplus value, Douglas explained how traditional capitalist methods of finance and capitalization assure that workers will never have enough money to fully afford the goods they produce, because much of that needed money is paid out as dividends to investors, or as interest to financiers and bankers. What remains to pay workers can never equal the full cost of producing the product, and therefore, since this "excess value" is being hoarded and kept out of circulation by the super-rich, the money available for consumption will always fall short of that needed to purchase the total goods and services produced. Hence, bottlenecks.

Hence the existence of shortages amidst plenty. Hence the need for foreign markets, the need to dump wheat or rice abroad while Americans are hungry.

It is this "siphoning off" and hoarding of money that bothered Pound so much. He considered it socially unhealthy and in a literal sense "unnatural." It was unhealthy in that a potato farmer, a cobbler, or a talented artist might work hard every day, making valuable contributions to the social good and yet be barely able to afford the necessities of life, while others who performed no useful service lived in luxury and sucked money from these workers in the form of dividends and interest. The system was "unnatural" in that it assigned to money a level of value that had no intrinsic connection with materials, with work, and with imagination, which Pound believed were the true measure of value.

> A work of art is no longer valued for the genius and vision that inhere in it, but because it can become a solid gold best-selling blockbuster.

Once true value is presumed to lie in money rather than in nature, in labor, in craft, a twisted and inverted value structure becomes inevitable. Land is no longer valued for its beauty or bounty but because it is a good investment. A shoemaker is no longer valued for the quality of his work but because he can produce a highly marketable commodity at a low price. A work of art is no longer valued for the beauty and vision that inhere in it, but because it can become a solid gold best-selling blockbuster.

And unlike a crop of potatoes or a pair of shoes, which have a distinct lifespan, money goes on forever. A potato rots. A pair of shoes wears out. But a dollar endures. And in fact grows, earns interest. We may think it humorous and eccentric that Imelda Marcos had hundreds of pairs of shoes in her closet. What would she ever do with them? we wonder. But we don't think it peculiar that she had many millions of dollars stashed away. We don't ask what she would do with all those dollars. And most of us will probably allow that J. R. Simplot is smart to sell his potatoes to McDonald's for cash, which he can keep in the bank or invest, whereas if he just kept the potatoes . . . well, what a stink.

Silvio Gessell was troubled by this tendency of money to endure and increase and accumulate in the hands of a few, and so he proposed a sort of temporary money, a money that would expire. It's an interesting notion, money that would exist only briefly like daffodils or plum blossoms. Imagine that the dollars you earned this morning would be good for two years. During that time you could buy anything you wanted, but at the end of that time, the money would be worthless paper. How would your life be different? Gessell—and also Pound—believed most people would spend their money, thus aiding in the transfer of goods and services. Great art works, fertile land, comfortable dwellings—these would become the repositories of wealth, and they would belong to those whose labors and talents contributed most to the general welfare of society.

So far as I know, this theory has never been thoroughly tested, just once for a brief period in Wörgel, Austria, during the 1930's. But even so, it seems to have crystallized in Pound's mind a belief that a great key to attaining social justice was the need to break up the huge concentrations of wealth, held in the form of currency by international banking cartels that knew no higher allegiance than their own self interest, which was always measured in monetary terms and attained by manipulating markets, exchange rates, and interest rates.

This is what Pound meant by *usury*, not strictly money lending, but avarice, the obsession with accumulating vast quantities of money, only to beget still more money. And when he wanted to personify usury, he reached deep into the European past—and into his own prejudiced past—for the image of the Shylock, the Jew.

This is what Pound meant by *usury*, not strictly money lending, but avarice, the obsession with accumulating vast quantities of money, only to beget still more money.

Those of us who have grown up in this country, and especially those who lived through World War II—or perhaps like me have a parent who fought in it—those who are aware of the nightmare of the Holocaust, may find it hard to imagine how Pound could have broadcast anti-American messages over Italian radio during the war years, especially since these messages, while often rambling and confused, were also strongly anti-Semitic. Pound believed the Allies, especially Roosevelt and Churchill, were owned by these financial cartels, run by "international Jewry."

Living in Italy, he watched the rise of Mussolini throughout the thirties. He believed "Muss," or "The Boss," as he liked to call him (yes, this was pre-Bruce Springsteen) was a man of action who genuinely cared about the welfare of his country. Pound equated Mussolini with Thomas Jefferson as a champion of agrarianism. Mussolini drained the swamps, creating an increased water supply and more arable land. He had battled the decadent Italian aristocracy, and Pound believed he would also stand up to the international bankers, munitions makers, and moneylenders, drive them from the temple, so to speak. In 1933, Pound met Mussolini, gave him a copy of *A Draft of XXX Cantos*, of which Muss is reported to have said, "*Ma questo . . . è divertante*." "But this . . . is amusing."

Pound was flattered, we might say "snowed," into believing Mussolini genuinely cared about the arts, and perhaps most importantly, into believing Mussolini took the poet and his economic ideas seriously—as no one in London or Washington would.

And it's here that the story turns tragic—in this tangled web of brilliance and naïveté, of noble intent and petty prejudice, of beautiful high art and bungling propaganda. Bitterly disillusioned with his homeland, feeling that he had no direct influence on American thought or policy, Pound reached for the platform he could obtain, and with his natural bent toward self-dramatization and his vitriolic diatribes against stupidity, greed, and laziness, he plunged ever deeper into his own incoherent outrage.

As early as the mid thirties, James Joyce, whose work Pound had helped advance, and for whom Pound had once bought a pair of good shoes to replace his old sneakers, began to think him obsessed. In his book *The Gift*, Lewis Hyde tells how Joyce, visiting Paris in 1935, thought "Pound was 'mad' and felt 'genuinely frightened of him.' Afraid to be alone with him, Joyce invited Hemingway to go with them to dinner; Hemingway found him 'erratic,' 'distracted.' Later T. S. Eliot also concluded that his friend had become unbalanced ('megalomania'), as did Pound's daughter, Mary ('his own tongue was tricking him, running away with him, leading him into excess, away from his pivot, into blind spots')" (245).

After the war, Pound was charged with treason, taken prisoner, and kept in a small metal cage at Pisa. Here, in the most appalling circumstance, he wrote some of his most beautiful and moving poetry. The *Pisan Cantos*, though charged with pain and anguish, have the delicate stillness of a storm just passed, of a reawakening to sunlight on water, to the small beauties and little kindnesses of people in adverse conditions. This is especially evident in the beautiful and haunting "Canto LXXXI," with its refrain, "Pull down thy vanity."

> The poems of this time have a quiet air of resignation and acceptance, tinged with regret, a reaching for the great crystal of light, an attempt to transcend and step beyond the trials and heartaches, the horror and pain that characterized so much of his later life.

In the end, for a variety of reasons, Pound was not tried for treason, but instead was diagnosed insane and placed in St. Elizabeth's hospital in Washington, DC, from 1946 to 1958. Upon his release, he returned to Italy. The poems of this time have a quiet air of resignation and acceptance, tinged with regret, a reaching for the great crystal of light, an attempt to transcend and step beyond the trials and heartaches, the horror and pain that characterized so much of his later life.

That he came at this point to acknowledge the extent to which his work had been ruined by his shallow and ill-tempered prejudice may help us grant his wish to be forgiven, but whether we consider that necessary, possible, or even desirable, I believe it's a good thing that we are here tonight in Pound's birthplace to honor what he in his better moments was trying to tell us, and also to understand how a man gifted with such talent, energy, and compassion could so lose his balance. Surely these are worthy purposes that can ennoble and enrich us and this community, while offering Ezra Pound the measure of tribute that he deserves.

The No Praise/No Blame Method:
A Process-based Writing Workshop

This writing workshop model involves students in all phases of the writing process. From prewriting and drafting through revising, students learn to share their efforts and to give formative, non-evaluative reader response that helps classmates move forward in their writing process.

The method has evolved gradually for me through years of teaching composition and creative writing classes. In composition classes, I was looking for ways to improve what we called, "peer editing sessions." I wanted to help students comment more effectively on each other's drafts, and I wanted to get students involved with each other's writing early in the writing process. As a result, I began blurring the line between peer editing sessions and "small group activities." Some activities might focus on invention or arrangement of the students' emerging essays, others on critical analysis of a published essay. Because the students in each group remained pretty much the same from one class session to the next, it was a small step from these collaborative activities to peer editing sessions. Having worked together discovering and shaping ideas, students understood the contexts in which their classmates' papers had been written. They knew about problems finding sources or reaching a conclusion, about sick children and heroic last minute writing binges. What they too often did not know was how to talk about the paper in ways that would help the writer.

> Having worked together discovering and shaping ideas, students understood the contexts in which their classmates' papers had been written.

Meanwhile, in my creative writing courses, instead of peer editing sessions, we had "workshops," whole class discussions of students' stories and poems, with me as facilitator. Here, often painfully and slowly, students learned the language of critique. They learned to do more than give a simple thumbs up or down. They learned to give comments that were complex, insightful, to show awareness of nuance and tone. And they learned to listen reflectively and attentively when their own work was discussed, to consider criticisms and suggestions for improving their writing.

The method melds the process-oriented small group approach of the composition classroom and the critique-oriented whole class approach of the creative writing workshop.

Yet this method, too, had limitations. The full class workshop, by nature, meant individual students could only hear their work discussed every two or three weeks, and then only at a late stage of the writing process when they had already committed a great deal to the piece and were often resistant to change. Also, the sheer amount of time required to give all students regular discussion of their writing left little time for anything else—little time to play with language, invent new poems, or discuss published poems. Working in small groups, however, students could get response to a poem, at some stage of development, in every workshop session.

So, just as I had earlier dissolved the boundary between peer editing sessions and small group workshops in my composition classes, I now began to dissolve the borders between my composition and my creative writing workshop methods. The resulting workshop melds the process-oriented small group approach of the composition classroom with the critique-oriented whole class approach of the creative writing workshop. The goals are to engage students constructively with each other's writing frequently and to create a continuing conversation that will help each student improve her writing from draft to draft.

The "no praise/no blame method" was invented, as far as I know, by William Stafford, who used it in a poetry workshop I attended, as a way to reduce competitiveness and defensiveness in our discussions of our poetry. The phrase echoes a Zen Buddhist expression (No praise. No blame. Just so.) and signifies simple acceptance, without judgment. Acknowledging that any honest effort at writing a poem had worth and value, Stafford avoided letting us get drawn into rating each other's poems, but rather directed our attention toward a poem's specific features—its lineation, its rhythms, its use of metaphor—encouraging us to give specific, constructive personal response that would help us see more clearly how our poems affected readers.

At about this same time, as I was fumbling and improvising my way along, I discovered Wendy Bishop's inspired and practical book, *Released Into Language*. In this book Bishop argues for a more process-oriented creative writing pedagogy, one that stresses the production of drafts as well as the critiquing of finished works. In this, she reaffirmed what I had already begun doing, and in her discussion of specific elements that might be included in such an approach, I discovered a section called "Full Group and Small Group Critique." Here she points out that both methods have advantages, small groups permitting students to try out ideas and responses in a "nonthreatening format" in which "even the shyest" student can participate. In contrast, large groups offer more opportunity "to gather and evaluate divergent opinions" as

> The phrase echoes a Zen Buddhist expression and signifies simple acceptance, without judging.

well as a greater "sense of the larger discourse community of professional writers"(53).

Later, in a chapter called "Revising and Responding," Bishop stresses the need to help students develop a process and vocabulary for their critique sessions: "if a teacher responds to student writing by saying 'it doesn't seem to have a center' and 'this bothers me' and 'this is interesting,' she should not be surprised to hear her students using the same imprecise response vocabulary" (143). Instead, drawing on the work of Peter Elbow and Pat Belanoff (Sharing and Responding, 1989), Bishop argues that we should teach students to vary their response types depending on the stage the writing is at, with early drafts perhaps receiving no response at all, and only later ones receiving a "criterion-based or judgment-based response" (144).

> I took bits and pieces from various workshops I had been in, combined them with some collaborative learning techniques, some reader response theory, and some popular transactional psychology.

Armed with my prior experiences and these new-found insights, I continued to experiment with small group workshops. In doing so, I took bits and pieces from various workshops I had been in, combined them with some collaborative learning techniques, some reader response theory, and some popular transactional psychology. The result was this method, which remains provisional and which I continue to refine and adapt for a wide range of composition and creative writing workshops, with groups ranging from basic writers to graduate students.

Early in the course, students are introduced to this method and taught to use it in whole class workshops. Typically, especially in an introductory class, we first use this method to discuss published works by established writers, or by student writers from a previous class, who have given permission to use their work. Besides considering the specific poems under discussion, we practice summarizing and asking questions that look beyond the writer's level of skill or the reader's predilections of taste, to matters of structure and theme, image and rhythm and voice. We relate the work to our own experiences and imaginations, expressing doubts and uncertainties as well as satisfactions. As we do, we develop attitudes, procedures, and vocabularies that will remain important when we focus on our own writing, first in whole class workshops, and later in small group workshops.

Once students begin to catch on, they can start using the method in small groups. Often students set the agenda, some sharing early drafts or even prewriting materials, while others bring revised versions of drafts that have already been discussed. Or I may have everyone do a quick discovery activity at the start of class and then discuss the results in small group workshops later in the period.

> Often students set the agenda, some sharing early drafts or even prewriting materials, while others bring revised versions of drafts that have already been discussed.

Though details of implementation vary widely depending upon the writing genre and the course level, the key principles remain intact:

1.) Drafts are shared throughout the writing process, sometimes in small groups, sometimes with the class a whole.

2.) Every piece discussed is "work in progress," and almost every draft can be improved with revision. The goal of the workshop is to help the writer revise successfully.

3) The first respondent to a draft gives a neutral, nonjudgmental summary—what Elbow and Belanoff call "sayback response"(SR 9).

3.) Other readers respond to the draft in ways that will help the writer see how the draft affects them.

4.) Readers speak to each other—not to the writer—about the draft while the writer listens quietly, perhaps taking notes.

5.) Readers try to acknowledge the subjective, personal element in their response, to say for instance, "I felt let down by the ending," rather than, "The ending is weak."

6.) The writer always gets the last word.

These are the essential elements of the process.

In calling this a "No Praise/No Blame Method" I don't want to convey that I think all writing equally excellent, or that there is no way to tell good writing from bad. On the contrary, I want to relocate the center of value from a hazy Platonic ideal of excellence to a "felt sense" of how the writing is valued by actual readers. To accomplish this, and to include what Elbow and Belanoff call "criterion–based feedback" (SR 11), I give students a set of criteria, which you'll find in *Figure 1* below. We discuss various criteria and how they might be evident in the poems, especially the published poems that we've been reading. And I encourage the students to consider and make explicit the qualities they most value in poetry.

I explain that the handout, which I regard as temporary and provisional and always subject to revision, represents my best attempt to tell them what I believe they should strive for in their writing. Still, like any such list, it is necessarily subjective, reflecting my own experiences and tastes. Another teacher would no doubt compose a different list. But here in this class where I am the teacher, these are my criteria, which I bring to the table and which I am always willing to reconsider.

To have such explicit criteria and at the same time to promote a No Praise/No Blame workshop model may appear contradictory: telling students to avoid judging or evaluating their classmates' writing while simultaneously holding my own evaluation criteria over everyone's head. But what I am really asking them to do is to suspend judgment, to downplay it, to keep it in perspective, and to see it in the context of this particular group. We all know quality matters. We all want to write the best papers, get A's, get published, win prizes, be on TV.

> But what I am really asking them to do is to suspend judgment, to downplay it, to keep it in perspective, and to see it in the context of this particular group.

But wait, back up, I'm trying to say. Forget all that stuff for a while and grant the writing simple acceptance, engage the words on the page, hear the writer's voice tremble as she reads through those lines about learning to dance. Forget where the poem might rate on some hypothetical scale of poetic quality and hear what the writer is saying, or almost saying, wanting to say, and help her find how to say it (Elbow and Belanoff SR25). Help her find ways to make the language fresher, the images sharper, the opening quicker. Let her know which lines unsettled you or made you laugh or confused you. Help her to see more clearly how the poem affected you. And encourage your classmates, other people in the group, to do the same. And the writer sits quietly listening.

In such a collaborative context, "students," in Kenneth Bruffee's words, "translate the language that they bring to the task into a composite working vocabulary common to the particular small group they are working in" (78-79). Further, as they return to the larger, whole class workshop, they learn to translate this small group vocabulary to that of a larger, more authoritative interpretive community represented by the instructor. It's a dynamic process in which terms, boundaries, values, theories, and beliefs are constantly discussed and redefined. But this isn't learning theory or even literary theory we're discussing here, it's poetry. And the most fundamental workshop goal is to create a supportive and non-threatening, yet challenging atmosphere in which students get deeply involved in writing and discussing drafts of their poems.

The process for discussing these drafts is outlined in *Figure 2* below. I've tried to make this handout straightforward and clear on the surface. Still, some attention to specific points may be warranted. First, I want to place the method in the context of reader response theory. I want writers to get a good sense of how the poem "lives" in the minds of its readers, and I want readers to attend not only to the poem, but to their own responses and how these responses are expressed to the group. It's not that I consider myself a reader response critic, but that I find this approach useful. Maybe that makes me a pragmatist. These are guidelines and suggestions, not rules, to help students respond effectively and constructively.

> It's not that I consider myself a reader response critic, but that I find this approach useful. Maybe that makes me a pragmatist.

The bulleted list at the top contains some general principles and thoughts that guide our discussions. Since these stress the writing's unfinished quality and the need for guidance and direction in revision, they are not too useful for discussions of published poems, though such speculations can prove interesting. Usually I briefly discuss points two and four, explaining that it's generally best to acknowledge the subjective element when you spot a problem and to ask other group members for their responses. Do other group members also have a problem with the ending, for instance? If so, how might it be solved (or "What if...?"), so that the discussion is extended and expanded, rather than shut down with a summary judgment.

The numbered list that follows outlines the basic process that we use whether in a large group or in small ones. It represents a synthesis of processes used in several workshops and writing groups that I've participated in. Key points here are one, two, three, six, and seven. We practice these points in the whole class workshops, and when students work in small groups, especially early in the term, I make a point to ensure that the process is followed, sometimes by eavesdropping, sometimes by sitting in on a group and modeling responses. Students especially like to skip point two, but I try to hold them to it, and eventually, usually after hearing a good summary of their own work, they come to appreciate its value.

> While the key principles remain the same, I often change individual elements.

The "conversation starters" at the bottom of the page are attempts to provide prompts, or cues, to revive a flagging discussion or shift direction without judging or evaluating. I wish I could tell you exactly where each of these prompts comes from, but I don't know that for sure. Some echo procedures recommended by Elbow and Belanoff. Others are comments I remember hearing in workshops or writing groups. A few sound like something salvaged from a couples' workshop. Perhaps something here is original, but I won't swear to it.

So that's the process and some of the rationale as it appears in a poetry writing class, especially an introductory class. I've also found the method useful in both composition and creative writing classes, at all levels. While the key principles remain the same, I often change individual elements. In more advanced classes, for instance, I often have the whole group generate the criteria sheet, first by proposing and discussing various criteria in small groups and then synthesizing and refining these in a group of the whole. Then, I'll type up and copy a final draft for them to keep in their notebooks. In an introductory workshop, I'll be more directive about both criteria and response procedures. Still whatever the class's level or genre, I've found this particular method blending composition and creative writing pedagogy allows me to create a classroom context that invites students to tap into a whole world of conversation that surrounds their writing.

Works Cited

Bishop, Wendy. Released into Language: Options for Teaching Creative Writing. Urbana: N.C.T.E., 1990.

Bruffee, Kenneth. *Collaborative Learning: Higher Education, Interdependence, and the Authority of Knowledge.* Baltimore: Johns Hopkins, 1993.

Elbow, Peter, and Pat Belanoff. *Sharing and Responding.* 2nd ed. New York: McGraw-Hill, 1995.

Figure 1:
Some Criteria for Judging Poetry

Our best poems —

- are authentic. *They come from a place inside of us that is real. They are spoken in our own voices and touch on matters that genuinely concern us.*

- give us back our lives. *They help us remember who we are and what we believe. In a world where we are continually pushed and pulled in a hundred directions by forces we sometimes only half understand, they help us stay centered and focused on what we most care about.*

- surprise us. *They use language in fresh and interesting ways. They offer unexpected insights and understandings into ourselves and each other. They offer new ways of imagining our potential as human beings.*

- touch the "poles of life." *They don't back away from difficult issues such as birth and death, peace and war, love and hate, elation and despair, the sacred and the profane, but they find ways of talking about these issues, and in doing so, they help us come to terms with essential parts of human experience that might otherwise be passed over alone and in silence.*

- make every word work. *They value language. They are high energy structures. Every word must earn its place in the poem. Every image must be necessary. If it doesn't add, it takes away: nothing is neutral.*

- grow out of concrete particulars. *They are made of the stuff of life. "No ideas but in things." Abstractions and generalizations work best in prose, not poetry. If used at all, they should be "earned." "For all the history of grief/an empty doorway and a maple leaf."--Archibald MacLiesh.*

- try to say what can't be said. *They test the possibilities of language by attempting to bring new areas of experience into awareness. Whether the writer is trying to resolve a paradox, to recreate a dream, or to discuss the death of a loved one, the poem* stretches to say what the writer didn't previously think could be said.

- contain a residue of mystery. *They are not quite paraphrasable or translatable. They evoke strong responses in their readers, but even after rereading and extensive discussion, there remains something elusive and mysterious that invites the reader back for another look.*

Figure 2:

No Praise/No Blame Workshop Guidelines

As you comment on one another's drafts, please keep the following points in mind:

- *These are not finished. Some roughness is expected.*
- *If you notice problems, call them to the writer's attention, but in a way that offers suggestions for revision.*
- *Try to understand the writer's goals. Don't try to make the poem or story into what you want it to be. Try to help make it into what the writer wants it to be.*
- *Point out strengths whenever possible. Make your comments specific. Point to particular passages and explain why they work well.*

In your discussions, please follow the procedure below as closely as possible:

> *1. Have the writer read the draft aloud while other group members jot down notes.*
>
> *2. Have one group member summarize the gist of the work—its central concern, striking features, dominant images, sources of tension, its crisis or turning point, etc.*
>
> *3. Have other group members comment on the summary, supplementing or modifying it.*

4. Have the writer reread the opening. What sort of tone does it establish? Does it invite further reading? Does it set up expectations of what will follow?

5. Have the writer reread the closing. Does it satisfy the expectations set up at the beginning? Does it leave you with a sense of satisfaction and completion?

6. Have the writer read a short passage from the heart of the work.

7. Ask the writer to comment and raise any questions that you haven't already covered.

Try these conversation starters:

- *Another way to look at it would be . . .*
- *I was most struck by . . .*
- *I think the writer wants to . . .*
- *This makes me feel . . .*
- *I wonder why . . .*
- *I want to hear more about . . .*
- *What if . . .*
- *Let's look more closely at . . .*
- *This reminds me of . . .*
- *So the point is . . .*

The Absolute Walking Its Planks:
Searching for C. K. Williams

To read C. K. Williams' early poems now that his later work, especially *Flesh and Blood*, is available is to be struck by the struggle of his poetic genius to locate its idiom and its *telos*. For while individual poems in earlier collections often do amazing things with language or open outward into striking psychological vistas, the gradual emergence of a complex and comprehensive poetic vision is especially compelling.

From this perspective, one of the most notable features of *Lies* (1969) is Williams' use of interior monologue as a genre that transcends psychology, re/presenting personal experience as an engrossing drama of fragmentation and reintegration, so that while speaking ostensibly to himself about issues generally kept private, Williams explores an inner world beyond the merely personal. From the particulars of experience, he reconstructs a state of mind we may all have known:

> *... the gradual emergence of a complex and comprehensive poetic vision is especially compelling.*

> *There is a world somewhere else that is unendurable.*
> *Those who live in it are helpless in the hands of elements,*
> *they are like branches in the deep woods in wind*
> *that whip their leaves off and slice the heart of night*
> *and sob. They are like boats bleating wearily in fog.*
>
> ("Dimensions")

Wait a minute . . . "wind / that whip"? Is this a typo, or what? It's hard, at first, to know for sure. Ah, yes, "branches" is the subject here, branches whip, but for an instant the dislocation creates doubt, and we, as readers, are briefly whipped by that wind, whipped into an alien land:

> And sometimes one of us, losing the way,
> will drift over the border and see them there, dying,
> laughing, being revived. When we come home, we are half way.
> Our screams heal the torn silence. We are the scars.

("Dimensions")

In his growing trust of such dislocations and his willingness to follow them, Williams begins to find both his voice and his vision. In this first collection, "Dimensions" and "On the Roof" reveal a speaker searching desperately for something to say, and for a way of saying it, some subjective correlative to the objective forces that torment him:

> In his growing trust of such dislocation and his willingness to follow it, Williams finds both his voice and his vision.

> Because even if I talk
> into my fist everyone hears my voice like the ocean
> in theirs, and so they solace me and I have to keep
> breaking toes with my gun-boots and coming up here
> to live—by myself, like an ariel, with a hand on the ledge,
> one eye glued to the tin door and one to the skylight.

("On the Roof")

Seen in this way, as they can be now that the later work is available, Williams' early poems clearly reveal the difficult, often painful struggle of his poetic genius to locate its voice and its goal.

Fragmentation or splitting of the self ("one eye glued to the tin door and one to the skylight") is a central theme in the collection and is especially evident in "Halves":

Halves

I am going to rip myself down the middle into two pieces
because there is something in me that is neither
the right half nor the left half nor between them.
It is what I see when I close my eyes, and what I see.

As in this room there is neither ceiling
nor floor, not space, light, heat or even
the deep skies of pictures, but something that beats softly
against others when they're here and others not here,

that leans on me like a woman,
curls up in my lap and walks
with me to the kitchen or out of the house altogether
to the street—I don't feel it, but it beats and beats;

so my life: there is this, neither before me
nor after, not up, down, backwards nor forwards from me.
It is like the dense sensory petals in a breast
that sway and touch back. It is like the mouth of a season,

the cool speculations bricks murmur, the shriek in orange,
and though it is neither true nor false, it tells me
that it is quietly here, and, like a creature, is in pain;
that when I ripen it will crack open the locks, it will love me.

> The effect has roots
> . . . also in the radical
> conceits of Donne
> and the English
> Metaphysicals . . .

This spectral haunting of the self by a presence that can only be known as absence, an elusive quintessence— terrifying and magnetic, dimly felt but never grasped or truly known— animates and binds the colliding images together even as they fight against each other. The effect has roots in surrealism, certainly, but also in the radical conceits of Donne and the English Metaphysicals, who sought a poetic style in which human consciousness could forge random and disparate elements of experience into a unified vision.

For Williams, however, the struggle takes place primarily in psychological rather than religious terms, and consciousness is something more complex and encompassing than mere reason. And so, if "Halves" is reminiscent of Donne's "Batter my heart, three-personed God," it is also very far from that poem in both sensibility and style. Just how far, however, cannot be seen until the poem is viewed in the context of Williams' later work.

I Am The Bitter Name, published in 1971, is an intensely political book, and in that respect an abrupt departure from *Lies*, published two years earlier. Yet the book is a departure in other less obvious ways as well, for while the almost Daliesque surrealism remains, as in "The Nickname of Hell," these poems burst forth urgently. They are not coaxed into being, but born of necessity.

Also, and this is crucial, Williams reaches much more directly into the realm of the profane for his central images and metaphors. In doing so, especially in combination with his expressions of horror and disgust at war and at corporate greed, he runs the risk of lapsing into mere irrationality and sensationalism. A lesser poet might have done so.

Yet where these poems are irrational, they are so in the good sense. That is, they step beyond the merely rational to expose its limitations. If their profanity sometimes feels sensational, it is because Williams understands, like Blake, that the sacred and profane are two halves of a whole, that no vision of life can be complete unless it takes both into account. As he asks in "In the Heart of the Beast," "if there was a way to purify the world who would be left?"

At its core, then, this collection is not a political statement but a religious/psychological drama like *The Book of Job* or Hopkins' "terrible sonnets." Sometimes an argument, sometimes a complaint, sometimes a benediction—the book swings rapidly, even violently, from one attitude to another as in the three poem sequence of "The Little Shirt," "Clay Out of Silence," and "Innings," each of which approaches spiritual concerns from a different but relatively coherent individual perspective. Yet the cumulative effect of all three is jarring.

> . . . the language balances horror and despair against peace and hope, unable to reconcile or transcend the polarities.

In "What Must I Do to Be Lost?" Williams leaps rapidly among images that suggest a broad range of emotional responses. This startling succession of images combines with wrenched syntax and a lack of punctuation to produce a hard-driving rhythm, simultaneously compelling and disorienting, until sound seems hopelessly at odds with sense, if there is sense here at all. Given the poem's title, however, this confusion can be seen as part of a necessary process, the process of becoming "lost," which itself cuts two ways: lost as abandoned, not of the elect; and lost as in the death of self, the dying of the personal ego, the individual will, into cosmic wholeness.

Here, as in so many of the other poems, the language balances horror and despair against peace and hope, unable to reconcile or transcend the polarities:

> *love pony darling let*
> *me be fields mines dry ditches*
> *my animal opens I*
> *sway I thrust aimlessly nothing*
> *is mine here*
> *take the knife I can't here*

swim in the thick break
me darling
I am in like a root
meat

("*What Must I Do to Be Lost?*")

From this fundamental need, this root sense of estranged
spiritual longing, the other poems radiate outward like
tendrils, extending into dreams, family, sexuality, politics,
friendship—drawing all of these concerns, and others as
well, into a collagelike pattern of correspondences and
interrelationships.

A full discussion of this collection, one that would do
justice to its boldness and complexity, would require a book
in itself. Not only would such a book have to explore the
underlying theology of the poems, a vision compounded of
"the hindu . . . the hebrew and the iliad" ("The Rampage"
2-3), but the ways these traditions were transformed and
personalized by the political and
psychological pressures of the 1960's.

In addition, the technical
sophistication of many poems is
dazzling. "Then the Brother of the
Wind," for instance, despite its lack of
punctuation, can be read as a single
sentence built out of an intricate

In addition,
the technical
sophistication of
many poems is
dazzling.

series of parallel constructions, each anchored by a key
term repeated with a slight twist so that the syntax gives a
sense of grammatical satisfaction, even while the metaphors
defeat understanding and pronoun referents become ever
more hazy, until in the final stanza the poem turns on itself
with a startling image that echoes backward to the first line,
in a sudden conjunction of grammatical, intellectual, and
emotional closure:

we'd still break like motors
and slip out of them anyway like penises
onto the damp thigh
and have to begin over

("Then the Brother of the Wind")

After such intensity, and especially after the brutal vision of "In the Heart of the Beast," *The Lark. The Thrush. The Starling. (Poems from Issa)* comes as a peaceful and gentle counterpoint. The extent to which these are direct translations of Issa (1763-1827) is difficult to determine. One poem is clearly based upon the burning of Issa's house shortly before his death in 1827, and another appears to refer to the untimely death of Issa's beloved daughter, Sato, but the voice is contemporary American, as are many of the sentiments. Clearly, the poems are not literal translations, but rather translations of a whole sensibility and culture.

To encounter these poems at this point is to feel as though a great storm has passed, a dark night ended, leaving behind destruction, yes, but also a hard-won tranquility. The poems move with deft precision and quiet grace. Figurative devices, especially the bold conceits of *I Am the Bitter Name,* take a back seat to clear, precise diction. Perplexity and anguish yield to wonder and reverence. Punctuation returns. It is as though Williams has broken through his doubt and dissociation to a calm, Zenlike way of living wholly in the moment—alive and accepting.

Like so much of the best of this kind of poetry, however, the apparent ease and simplicity are deceptive, as is the suggestion that this is a collection of individual poems rather than a single extended meditation. For while it is true that

each poem has a *waka*-like autonomy and integrity that could
allow it to stand alone, it is also true that each piece depends
on the others and on its place in the overall sequence for much
of its force. Thus, they appear to be linked sequentially in the
manner of *renga*. The last poem, "Did I write this," for example,
could not have the same impact in the middle of the sequence.
In fact, individually, these poems, despite their penetrating
insights, offer only brief, intriguing glimpses rather than
opening up a whole way of seeing. Read in sequence, however,
they play off of each other and build a loosely connected web,
touching at one point upon kneading dough:

> *So*
> *mucked up with*
> *kneading*
> *dough she is*
>
> *she has to use*
> *her wrist to*
> *push her hair back*
> *from her eyes.*

At another point upon meditation and language:

> *Listen carefully.*
>
> *I'm meditating.*
> *The only thing in my mind*
> *right now*
> *is the wind.*
>
> *No, wait . . . the autumn*
> *wind, that's right,*
> *the autumn wind!*

At another upon killing a cockroach:

> *What a sound his*
> *shell made, that*
> *big cockroach!* Crack!
> *like a churchbell:*

Crack!
Crack!
Crack!

Finally, we may be tempted to wonder, as he does in the final poem:

Did I write this
as I was
dying?

Did I really
write
this?

That I wanted to thank
the snow
fallen on my blanket?

Could I
have written
this?

How different this is from Williams' earlier work, and yet how appropriate—and how impossible without that earlier work.

In an important sense, *The Lark. The Thrush. The Starling.* is less a departure for Williams than a point of transition, as though he has finally taken a very deep breath, settled down, and begun to find a stance and a voice to carry him beyond the abyss he seemed to be falling through in *I Am the Bitter Name*. It would no doubt be an over-simplification to attribute this entirely to involvement with Zen, but nevertheless, he appears to have experienced a significant spiritual breakthrough between *I Am the Bitter Name* and *With Ignorance*.

> How different this is from Williams' earlier work, and yet how appropriate—and how impossible without that earlier work.

With Ignorance, published in 1977, veers away from minimalism, back toward the complexity and inclusiveness of earlier collections but, as the title implies, with a new humility, and as significantly, with a deeper and stronger sense of self— no longer the lonely, fragmented ego casting desperately about for, yet simultaneously rejecting, solace, but the deeply felt sense of participation in a vast cosmic drama at once absurd and holy, reality and illusion. Williams has also found a longer line and a new discourse mode, combining narrative with interior monologue. Taken together, all these factors help him to sustain a longer poem while holding its center with a controlling and unquestionably authentic voice.

> On the one hand, they are much more direct and straightforward than the earlier ones, and so require less explication.

These qualities are evident throughout, but nowhere more so than in "The Last Deaths," a poem that demands to be read in its entirety. In fact, the whole question of how to discuss these poems is extremely problematic. On the one hand, they are much more direct and straightforward than the earlier ones, and so require less explication. At the same time, they are so sophisticated rhetorically and so rich in imagery and human understanding that, despite their length, one wants to savour every word.

"The Last Deaths" begins casually, even prosaically, "A few nights ago I was half-watching the news on television and half-reading to my daughter." It goes on to recount a bit of the book's story, intercut with glimpses of the news, punctuated by Jessie's (the daughter's) question, "What's the matter with her? Why's she crying?" Next, the speaker interrupts himself to explain, "I haven't lived with my daughter for more than a year now and sometimes it still hurts not to be with her more . . .. I don't see her often enough to be able to know what I can say to her, / what I can solve for her without introducing more confusions than there were in the first place."

He retells a story about acquainting her with the concept of death, reminding himself of how hard it is for her to come to terms with such matters, and yet how much she needs an honest and clear explanation of this incident she has seen on television—a woman wracked with grief because her husband and children have been slaughtered by soldiers. Unable to speak frankly to Jessie, he speaks to himself in an interior monologue:

> *These times. The endless wars. The hatred. The vengefulness.*
> *Everyone I know getting out of their marriage. Old friends*
> *   distrustful.*
> *The politicians using us until you can't think about it anymore*
> *   because you can't tell anymore*
> *which reality affects which and how do you escape from it without*
> *   everything battering you back again?*

He imagines himself addressing Jessie, speaking the tangled truth as he understands it:

> *Last night while you and that poor woman were trading deaths like*
> *   horrible toys,*
> *I was dreaming about the universe. The whole universe was*
> *   happening in one day, like a blossom,*
> *and during that day people's voices kept going out to it crying,*
> *   "Stop! Stop!"*
> *The universe didn't mind, though. It knew we were only cursing*
> *   love again*
> *because we didn't know how to love, not even for a day,*
> *but our little love days were just seeds it blew out on parachutes*
> *   into the summer wind. . . .*
> *and whatever our lives were, our love, this once, was enough.*

Finally, the poem's statement is affirmative and redemptive, suffused with a sort of innocence even, but innocence tempered by fire, far removed from, and inaccessible to, the naïveté of childhood.

Maybe the best way to capture the flavor of this book is simply to quote a few opening lines:

> *If you put in enough hours in bars, sooner or later you get to hear*
> *every imaginable kind of bullshit.*
>
> *("Bob")*
>
> *This is a story. You don't have to think about it, it's make-believe.*
>
> *("Near the Haunted Castle")*
>
> *When I was about eight, I once stabbed somebody, another kid,*
> *a little girl.*
>
> *("Blades")*
>
> *Again and again. Again lips, again breast, again hand, thigh, loin*
> *and bed and bed.*
>
> *("With Ignorance")*

From each of these points, Williams launches into a poem that is as much meditation as story, as much a consideration of *how* we know as a revelation of *what* we know.

Tar (1983) offers an extension and refinement of the themes and techniques introduced in *With Ignorance* rather than a radical departure. Still writing with the longer line that served him well in the previous collection, he continues to work primarily with narrative monologues, and as in *With Ignorance*, he concludes with a long poem of sustained reflection and speculation. To note that the similarities between these two collections are more numerous than between any two others, however, is not to diminish the importance of *Tar*. Besides containing several remarkable narratives—"The Gift," "The Color of Time," "Combat," "Still

... innocence tempered by fire, far removed from, and inaccessible to, the naïveté of childhood.

Life," and "The Gas Station"—in "One of the Muses" *Tar* offers an invaluable personal exploration of Williams' relation to his poetry.

Part biography, part psychology, part literary theory, "One of the Muses" resembles, on a much smaller scale, Wordsworth's *The Prelude* in the way it attempts to trace out the various forces that have shaped the poet's sensibility, while at the same time showing those forces in action in the poem itself. Beyond this general similarity in intent and method, however, the two works are as different as the poets who wrote them.

Williams' two epigraphs, taken from Plato and Wittgenstein, announce that this poem is concerned less with biography than with the spring from which the poetic impulse arises. That Williams conceives of this well-spring as a sort of ungrounded absolute reality is not surprising, given the spiritual longing that animates many of his strongest poems. Nevertheless, to speak intelligently and comprehensibly about such ultimate concerns remains inordinately difficult. How does one speak of the formless? Williams' answer is to adopt the conventional symbol of the muse, or more specifically *one* of the muses, as a representation, pointing beyond herself so that as Wittgenstein says, "language suggests a body and there is none":

> Here in a relatively stable present, no cries across the gorge, no veils
>   atremble,
> it sometimes seems as though she may have been a fiction utterly,
>   a symbol or a system of them.

In any case, what good conceivably could come at this late date
of recapitulating my afflictions?

("One of the Muses")

His answer to that question is simply that "it's to be accounted
for, that's all." And in the process of giving this accounting,
Williams presents his evolving relationship with this muse
much in the manner of a love affair, from her first appearance
to him in a period of spiritual doubt,
through their soaring consummation
which "came to seem a myth, a primal
ceremony," followed by doubts and
misgivings, her disdainful turning
from him in silence, intermittent
returns when she "left her cleft of
reticence ajar: a lace, a latticework." As
their relationship deepens, he grows
increasingly frustrated by the disparity between his needs for
her and her cool remoteness, until anguished and bereft, he
turns back upon himself:

> *Wherever I did find the strength, half of it I dedicated to absolving*
> *   and forgiving her.*
> *Somehow I came to think, and never stopped believing, I was*
> *   inflicting all my anguish on myself.*
> *She was blameless, wasn't she? Her passivity precluded else:*
> *   the issue had to be with me.*

Consumed in abandonment and guilt, he begins to exhaust
his internal resources and finally feels himself going mad. At
last, in the depths of his madness, he experiences the birth of
a second mind (it is interesting to read "Halves" and "Then the
Brother of the Wind" in this context), which troubled as it is,
offers a sort of meta-perspective from which he can view his
original "sane" mind:

> At last, in the depths of his madness, he experiences the birth of a second mind . . .

I knew already that my other mind—I could hardly recall it—
  had a flaw and from that flaw
had been elaborated a delusion, and that delusion, in its turn
  was at the base of all my suffering,
all the agonies I'd been inflicting, so unnecessarily, I understood,
  upon myself.

From this fresh perspective, he starts to build a new epistemology, in which he is truly a creator or maker of reality rather than a mere scribe recording sense impressions. The result is an exhilarating sense of power and fulfillment, until even this leaves and he arrives in a new place:

Somehow, I knew I'd touched the very ground of self, its axioms
  and assumptions,
and what was there wasn't what I'd thought—I hadn't known
  what I'd thought but knew it now—

He returns to himself feeling shy and somewhat estranged, but sure and trusting, recognizing that the muse is now gone for good and he will have to make his way without her. The earlier sense of abandonment and desolation has also gone, however, replaced by "the certainty that something was attained."

Finally, in a startlingly beautiful conclusion, he speculates that she may be the poetry itself, "what she herself effected" —both cause and effect, that which is embodied in language and that which language can only suggest, "precisely scored—no rests, diminuendos, decrescendos—silencing, and silence."

From this fresh perspective, he starts to build a new epistemology, in which he is truly a creator or maker of reality rather than a mere scribe recording sense impressions.

In many ways a reflective analysis of the pressures and discoveries that have shaped his poetry over the past twenty years, "One of the Muses" can also be seen as an interpretive key to the poems.

It offers a reconstruction of Williams' journey into and beyond the self. Yet, in many ways, it is incomplete, necessarily so, for the terror and magnificence of this journey, the horror and beauty, lie in the traveling—and finally in the courage and imagination of the traveler. "One of the Muses" may serve as a roadmap into this strange and magnificent dimension, but it is only that. Those who want more than a roadmap, will have to read *Flesh and Blood*.

In *Flesh and Blood*, Williams offers both refinement and departure. As in earlier collections, he moves freely between the mundane and the metaphysical, but now appears to do so in concert with rather than at the mercy of some "muse" or *daimon* beyond his control. The long lines and discursive style characteristic of *With Ignorance* and *Tar* remain, but are now held firmly within the bounds of an eight-line unit— sometimes comprised of an individual poem, sometimes part of a multi-poem sequence, sometimes eight-line stanzas within a single long poem. Within this consistent eight-line unit, Williams composes in open-ended, speculative sentences that play with syntax, semantics, and sound as they search out their arc of completion. The result is a tempering, at once strengthening and seasoning the work with hard-won spiritual, psychological, and technical assurance.

Although the book's three parts share similarites in voice, subject matter, and form, each section has a dominant signature, or motif. Part I, by far the longest, ranges widely over a variety of subjects from "Fast Food" to "Drought" to "Religious Thought." Despite an occasional pair of complementary poems ("Snow: I" and "Snow: II," for instance) or a more loosely knit group ("Artemis," "Herakles," "Medusa,"

"Midas"), the poems do not connect tightly but rather play upon or against each other with collagelike juxtapositions: the concrete against the abstract, the personal against the political, the tragic against the comic, the beautiful against the grotesque.

Yet the form, due to its very regularity, becomes almost invisible, a stable undercurrent to the pointed observations of the ordinary drama of everyday reality—the woman on the subway with hooks for hands, the lesbian couple in the park with their daughter, Bishop Tutu's visit to Reagan at The White House, the nature of Modernism, the magnificent terror of divine madness. And it is this last, this terror—at once compelling and overwhelming—that sounds the dominant theme of Part I.

> ... the pointed observations of the ordinary drama of everyday reality— the woman on the subway with hooks for hands, the lesbian couple in the park with their daughter, Bishop Tutu's visit to Reagan at The White House ...

"Religious Thought" captures this feeling well. The title, for instance, can be read in at least two relevant ways: "Religious" may be a restrictive modifier, suggesting that of all one's thoughts some few may be religious and those few are about to be discussed, or the modifier may be non-restrictive, in which case the title would imply that "Thought" itself may be a religious activity, an encounter with the incomprehensible:

> Beyond anything else, he dwells on what might inhabit his mind
>   at the moment of his death,
> That which he'll take across with him, which will sum his being up
>   as he's projected into spirit.
> Thus he dwells upon the substance of his consciousness,
>   what its contents are at any moment:
> good thoughts, hopefully, of friends, recent lovers, various
>   genres of attempted bliss. . . .

His secret is the terror that mind will do to him again what it did
   that unforgivable once.
Sometimes, lest he forget, he lets it almost take him again: the vile
   thoughts, the chill, the dread.

Precariously balanced between affirmation and negation, he
is drawn in both directions, wishing to choose affirmation
yet knowing that the choice of negation is also profound and
compelling. The poem clearly hearkens back not only to "One
of the Muses," but to "Halves":

because there is something in me that is neither
the right half nor the left half nor between them.
It is what I see when I close my eyes, and what I see.
. . .

and though it is neither true nor false, it tells me
that it is quietly here, and, like a creature, is in pain;
that when I ripen it will crack open the locks, it will love me.

And perhaps a ripening *has* taken place, for although various
poems skirt the edges of that terror, letting "it almost take
him again," they do not plunge into the abyss. Instead, they
probe, almost toy with the terror of seeing too deeply and
speaking too clearly. A tension that could otherwise become
unbearable is characteristically de-fused—sometimes, as
in "The Body," with sympathetic humor, sometimes, as in
"Blame," with "a gesture of just-fathomable irony."

   "Dawn," the final poem of Part I, explores the texture of
a particular morning, a brief interval of "mist" and "sea fog"
in a time of "unwavering heat" and "overpowering sunlight."
For the briefest moment, a bit of the sea fog gathers in the
branches of "the drought-battered spruce on its lonely knoll."
A sparrow lands, "swaying precipitously on a drop-glittering
twiglet." It is joined by a another bird, then a third, unseen
but singing out of "that dim, fragile, miniature cloud," which
is already burning off in the stark light of day. Like the poet

himself, that solitary spruce hangs on to life, and for an instant at least is inhabited by an obscure spirit that fills its weary branches with song.

> Like the poet himself, that solitary spruce hangs on to life, and for an instant at least is inhabited by an obscure spirit that fills its weary branches with song.

The thirty three poems in Part II are gathered into five groups: "Reading," "Suicide," "Love," "Good Mother," and "Vehicle." Grouped thus, individual poems are much more tightly knit into sequences than those in Part I, so that they maintain their autonomy while also functioning as part of a larger whole and offering chances for more extended exploration of a subject than would be possible within a single eight line poem. The three poems on suicide, for instance, offer varied perspectives on that final and irrevocable act of negation—self-destruction.

The first poem, "Suicide: Elena," reflects on the death of a former client in one of Williams' psychotherapy groups. Clearly moved by the suicide of this thin, vulnerable fourteen and a half year old girl, Williams asks a boy if he knew her, only to have the boy correct his mispronunciation of the girl's name, thereby underlining the sense of helplessness and distance. "Suicide: Ludie," second in the sequence, stretches the distance even farther. A pay phone is ringing. Williams answers it. A voice asks for Ludie. When told "there isn't anybody around here," the voice replies, "Well, what am I supposed to do? What are you supposed to do when somebody's gonna kill herself?" / "The police. Where does Ludie live?" "That's the whole thing, she don't *live* where she lives." And so the poem ends, offering a shallow ironic satisfaction with its play on *"live,"* yet undercutting this with a deep sense of isolation and helplessness.

Finally, "Suicide: Anne," dedicated to Anne Sexton,
attempts to understand the forces, the needs and pressures,
that might drive a person to take her life:

> *Perhaps it isn't as we like to think, the last resort, the end*
> *   of something, thwarted choice or attempt,*
> *but rather the ever-recurring beginning, the faithful first*
> *   to that very image of endeavor,*
> *so that even the most patently meaningless difficulties,*
> *   a badly started nail, a lost check,*
> *not to speak of the great and irresolvable emotional issues,*
> *   would bring instantly to mind*
> *that unfailingly reliable image of a gesture to be carried out*
> *   for once with confidence and grace.*

If this poem does not adequately settle the difficult, perhaps
irresolvable issues raised by the previous two, it does provide
a sense of closure to the sequence. The same isolation that
leaves us feeling so distraught and helpless when confronted
by a suicide accentuates both our fundamental aloneness—
our final inability to comprehend the
full range of another person's needs,
desires, and motives—and also our
need to try. The bungled conversation
with Elena's friend, the desperate
phone call about Ludie, the shape of
Anne Sexton's mind and heart in a
body of poems—all help in different
ways to fill that need for community
and understanding, but are all finally
inadequate, "as though the pestering
forces of inertia that for so long had
held you back had ebbed at last / and you could slip through
now, not to peace particularly, not even to escape, but to
completion."

As in other sequences, each poem resembles a window through which the reader is permitted to view an event or phenomenon from different angles, gaining each time a fuller understanding, but realizing all the while that the subject in its totality remains slightly elusive, that only by being both inside and outside the room while simultaneously looking through every possible window could the phenomenon be fully apprehended, if even then.

In Part III, Williams continues working in an eight line unit, but here the sequence is bound so tightly together that the eighteen pieces come together into a single long poem, "Le Petit Salvié," an elegy for friend and fellow poet, Paul Zweig, who died in 1984 after an excruciating battle with lymphoma. The parts are interdependent, relying on each other and on their place in the poem's overall movement for most of their force. A few, such as numbers 8 and 9, are sufficiently self contained to stand alone, but even these gain resonance when read in the overall context. Still, the interdependence is a matter of degree, and raises questions about the point at which a tightly knit sequence of poems becomes an individual work.

> . . . only by being both inside and outside the room while simultaneously looking through every possible window could the phenomenon be fully apprehended, if even then.

"Le Petit Salvié" is both a deeply felt personal tribute and an extended meditation on human mortality. The central fact of Zweig's death lends concrete immediacy to thoughts that might otherwise seem abstract and remote. Conversely, the meditative speculation contextualizes and universalizes the personal grief. In many ways, working through that grief becomes a structural principle. From memories of Zweig's final days and even moments, Williams shifts the focus to his

own sense of loss and doubt: "In my
adult mind, I'm reeling, lost—I can't
grasp anymore what I even think of
death. / I don't know even what we
hope for: ecstasy? bliss? or just release
from being, not to suffer anymore." The
impact of Zweig's death upon those
closest to him, his daughter Genevieve

Conversely,
the meditative
speculation
contextualizes and
universalizes the
personal grief.

and Vikki Stark, is set against a view that alludes to John
Donne's "Death Be Not Proud." Perhaps Zweig has defeated
death and is *not* dead:

> *If you're accessible to me, how can you be dead? You are*
> *accessible*
>   *to me, therefore . . . something else.*
> *So what I end with is the death of death, but not as it would*
>   *have been elaborated once,*
> *in urgencies of indignation, resignation, faith: I have you*
>   *neither here, nor there, but not not-anywhere:*
> *the soul keeps saying that you might be here, or there—*
>   *the incessant passions of the possible.*

The loss is real, the grief is real, yet so is the reality of having
once been touched by Zweig's life, the continuing presence of
his memory, of his work:

> *There are no consolations, no illuminations, nothing of that*
>   *long-awaited flowing toward transcendence.*
> *There is, though, compensation, the simple certainty of having*
>   *touched and having been touched.*
> *The silence and the speaking come together, grief and gladness*
>   *come together, the disparates fuse.*

However we may construe these disparates—as life and death,
grief and joy, abstract and concrete, relative and absolute, self
and other, spirit and matter—their fusion offers a resolution
to the grief expressed earlier, as well as to the poem:

Farewell your dumb French farmer's hat, your pads of yellowed
       paper, your joyful, headlong scrawl.
The coolness of the woods, the swallow's swoop and whistle,
       the confident call of the owl at night.
Scents of dawn, the softening all-night fire, char, ash, warm embers
       in the early morning chill.
The moment holds, you move across the path and go, the light lifts,
       breaks: goodbye, my friend, farewell.

And so it must be for us all in the end, but this sense of life's ending embraces those conflicting thoughts and feelings in a clear-eyed, straightforward statement of acceptance that requires no explication.

Imaginative Options:
Some Other Ways to Write about Literature

*No sooner have you feasted on beauty with your eyes
than your mind tells you that beauty is vain and that
beauty passes. Death, oblivion, and rest lap round your
songs with their dark wave. And then, incongruously,
a sound of scurrying and laughter is heard. There is
a patter of animals' feet and the odd guttural notes
of rooks and the snufflings of obtuse furry animals
grunting and nosing. For you were not a pure saint by
any means. You pulled legs; you tweaked noses. You were
at war with all humbug and pretence.*

—*Virginia Woolf*

In this passage from "I Am Christina Rossetti," an essay marking the centenary of Rossetti's birth, Virginia Woolf abruptly breaks from writing *about* Rossetti and addresses the poet directly in a striking apostrophe. Reading this, I am reminded how easily writers speak across time. We know, of course, that writers from past times speak to us here in the present, but can we reply? Why not? Can they hear us? Who can say for sure? But whether they hear us is not the point; such apostrophes have a second audience in mind, an *indirect* audience. While ostensibly speaking directly to Christina Rossetti, Woolf also creates a new rhetorical context in which her readers become an indirect audience, eavesdroppers on a bit of overheard conversation: one writer speaking frankly to another.

> Reading this, I am reminded of how easily writers can speak across time.

> Yes, real writers can do this, beautifully and memorably. But students?

Sure, "real" writers can do this sort of thing. William Wordsworth, for instance, in his sonnet, "London: 1802," when he says, "Milton, thou shoulds't be living at this hour, / England hath need of thee" or W. H. Auden in Part 2 of "In Memory of W. B. Yeats," when he addresses the poet, saying, "Mad Ireland hurt you into poetry. / Now Ireland has her madness and her weather still, / For poetry makes nothing happen . . . ." Yes, real writers can do this, beautifully and memorably. But students?

Here is Brandon, a student in my Survey of British Literature class writing to Wilfred Owen about his poem, "*Dulce et Decorum Est*":

> *Finally, the bitterness of war and fighting is truly brought out in the last two lines of the poem: "To children ardent for some desperate glory, / The old Lie: Dulce et decorum est pro patria mori." I understand this line completely. Every government and national leader fills all of their country's young people with the notion that it is very honorable to die for one's country. Then all of these people have a high morale going into a war until they actually realize that war is a gruesome, horrible experience that nobody should have to endure. That, my friend, is why you stated this was a complete lie. I will take your word for it because you never made it out of World War I. . . . I offer much respect to you and every other that has served his country. That, my friend, is not a lie. I just wrote to tell you how much I enjoyed and ingested your poem. Please write back soon.*

No, this is not Virginia Woolf or W. H. Auden writing. It's Brandon, struggling with poetry, struggling with language and ideas and emotions. And Brandon's letter, from which this is excerpted, has some rough spots, but Brandon writes with voice, with conviction, with a strong sense of audience and purpose. I enjoy reading such papers, and since I have about forty students in each survey class, that enjoyment counts for a lot.

But it's not just *my* enjoyment that I'm thinking of; I'm also trying to make this assignment enjoyable for the students, most of whom are not English majors and have little need to practice the scholarly conventions of literary discourse.

Students in my British literature survey classes may write a traditional critical or research-based essay. Or if they prefer, they may use an *imaginative option* to respond to and show their understanding of the works we are reading. I encourage them to write creatively about literature using a variety of genres—journals, interviews, letters, poems, dramas, lesson plans, and more. Although I make clear that I have no preference which option they take, generally about half choose non traditional approaches. In a recent batch of papers, for instance, I received letters to friends, spouses, and parents discussing the poetry of William Blake, William Wordsworth, and Samuel Taylor Coleridge. I received letters to and about Mary Wollstonecraft and read an interview with her on *Oprah's Book Club*. I also received one Italian sonnet in the manner of Keats, accompanied by supplementary discussion, and one short poem written in Spenserian stanzas, and modeled on Byron's "Childe Harold's Pilgrimage."

> I encourage students to write creatively about literature using a variety of genres—journals, interviews, letters, poems, dramas, lesson plans, and more.

Many students also write more traditional critical/ analytical papers. Most often, these explore topics developed from in-class freewrites and discussions. And because two papers are required per semester, individual students often opt to write one paper of each type.

At this point, I may as well confess that I come to this approach from a somewhat eclectic academic background. In graduate school, I studied literature. In fact, for my doctorate I wrote a dissertation on the metaphysical poetry of Henry Vaughan. Enjoyable and rewarding as this was, however, it didn't help me find a tenure-track job. As a result, I spent several years teaching and studying composition as an adjunct instructor.

> I started talking about William Blake in my nonfiction class, about free writing in my British Survey, about cumulative sentence structure in my poetry class. And, it was okay.

And instead of writing about metaphysical poetry, I began to write and publish my own poems. I also wrote a composition textbook and a few articles on teaching writing, all of which, back in those days before Ph.D.'s in rhetoric were common, qualified me as a composition teacher. Because the Boise State University English Department, then as now, was often short staffed due to sabbaticals or budgetary holdbacks, I sometimes taught creative writing classes and literature surveys, along with expository writing classes.

Moving back and forth among these areas, I tried to keep their subjects and methods strictly compartmentalized, to color within the lines. But it wasn't easy. I understood there was no time to teach writing in a literature class, no time to teach literature in a composition class. And creative writing? Well, that was another world entirely. And so it went: 9:15, Nonfiction Writing; 10:40, Survey of British Literature Since 1790; 12:15, Advanced Poetry Writing—like Herb Philbrick, the protagonist of a TV show I watched as a child, *I Led Three Lives*.

In my survey classes at that time, writing assignments conformed roughly to the proportions that Wendy Bishop observed in introductory literature courses: 15% *Exploratory* (reader-response journals, position papers, drafts of interpretations); 80% *Instrumental* (biographical essays, critical essays, book reviews, etc.); 5% Imaginative (imitations, creative writing options) (36). Gradually, however, this pattern began to change. I started talking about William Blake in my nonfiction class, about free writing in my British Survey, about cumulative sentence structure in my poetry class. And, it was okay. I saw that beyond the categorical boundaries imposed by curricular design, woven deeply into the fabric of my teaching and learning experience, was a rich interpenetration of subject and method that I could tap into in my teaching, and in my writing. The lines between literature, creative writing, and composition began to look more like shared borders.

Even so, I sensed a need for more system and method. One especially helpful essay was "Literature, Composition, and the Structure of English" by Nancy R. Comely and Robert Scholes. They believe that

> *a writing approach to literary texts, in which students write in the forms they are reading or use such texts as intertexts for writing in other forms, not only will improve their ability to write in all forms of discourse, but will also improve ability to read and interpret texts. (108)*

Among their examples of such writings are updating the slang in Gwendolyn Brooks's "We Real Cool" from a 1950's feel to a more contemporary idiom (107). Another is to write from the viewpoint of Edwin Arlington Robinson's Richard Cory, just before he "went home and put a bullet through his head"(105).

To integrate writing assignments with classroom learning activities, I often devote class time to informal exploratory writings that students share and discuss.

In my overall philosophy and my classroom method, I am deeply indebted to both Wendy Bishop and James Britton. Much of Bishop's pedagogy is built upon the work of Britton, especially upon his three major categories of writing function: the *Expressive*, the *Transactional*, and *the Poetic* (*Development* 81-86). Expressive writing, broadly, is writing that is informal, "close to the self," "thinking aloud on paper." Transactional writing is done to "inform people . . ., to advise or persuade or instruct people." Poetic writing, in contrast, "uses language as an art medium" (*Development* 88-91). Bishop's three types of discourse, noted above, are based upon Britton's model, with her term "Exploratory" being roughly equivalent to Britton's "Expressive," her "Instrumental" equivalent to Britton's "Transactional," and her "Imaginative" equivalent to his "Poetic" (29). I like Bishop's terms because they emphasize the ways this discourse taxonomy plays out in teaching.

To integrate writing assignments with classroom learning activities, I often devote class time to informal exploratory writings that students share and discuss. See *Figure 1*. An activity like this one typically takes about 40 minutes. First I distribute the topics and read them aloud, then ask the students to pick one and free write on it for about ten minutes. I tell them they will not have to show this to anyone or turn it in, but the writing will help them explore, extend, and solidify their thoughts before discussing them in a small group. And I also point out that the freewrites, and the ideas that come up in the ensuing discussions, could be useful for one of the required papers or for answering an essay question on an exam. A frequent variant of this activity is to have students bring to class a list of four questions about a work—Coleridge's "Chistabel," for instance—and then in a group of four persons, use a process of synthesis and selection to narrow the sixteen questions from each group to four that will be shared with the whole class.

As the due date for papers approaches, I remind the class that they have been accumulating a number of interesting issues and ideas (Expressive/Exploratory writings) that could be explored more fully in a critical essay (Transactional/ Instrumental writing) or a creative piece (Poetic/Imaginative writing). Also, to help students envision some of the things they might do for an imaginative paper, I often make a point of directing their attention to works like those noted above by Woolf, Wordsworth, and Auden. Or in connection with Coleridge's "Kubla Khan," we will read Stevie Smith's poem "Thoughts On the Person From Porlock." Along with Marlowe's "The Passionate Shepherd to His Love," we read Ralegh's "The Nymph's Reply to the Shepherd" and Donne's "The Bait." But these are only some obvious instances from British Survey. Other possibilities will spring to mind for teachers of other courses. Such examples show students that such writing can have value and purpose beyond just satisfying a class requirement.

> Because such diverse submissions can prove difficult to evaluate, I have evolved a set of broadly applicable grading criteria, which I distribute early in the term.

Because such diverse papers can prove difficult to evaluate, I have evolved a set of broadly applicable grading criteria, which I distribute early in the term. See *Figure 2*. This handout helps students see what I am looking for. A few sample criteria are:

- How much time, effort, and imagination appear to have gone into this?
- Does this show a good understanding of the literature we've been studying?

By making criteria known early and applying them consciously when grading, I've been able to overcome many difficulties in evaluating such a varied group of writing projects.

Student response to this approach has been positive. They like being able to do either a traditional essay or take an imaginative option. This is reflected in their informal comments, their course evaluations, and especially the projects themselves. And in this paper about student writing, it seems appropriate to close with another example. Here are a few excerpts from Meagan's letter to Virginia Woolf, inspired by the essay, "Professions for Women," and offering a twenty first century take on "The Angel in the House":

I am dealing with a different Angel, however, but one very similar to the one you were able to conquer. . . . She is the Angel of the Workplace, and she has chosen to follow me, bringing with her promises of wealth, of fancy cars, and designer clothing. . . .

Virginia, our angels seem to come from two opposite sides. Is it the plight of woman always to have an angel on her back of some sort or another? Just how were you able to kill the Angel of the House? It had to have been more than a tossed inkpot in her direction more than once. In your writing, you said that the "struggle was severe." I can only hope that my struggle will end as yours did and that the Angel will quit appearing everywhere, even on the lips of my future mother-in-law! When something is that persistent, it seems almost impossible to destroy. Writing to you has helped somewhat to clarify my perspective of the angel. In closing I will borrow from your "Professions for Women": "My time is up, and I must cease."

Works Cited

Bishop, Wendy. *Released into Language: Options for Teaching Creative Writing.* Urbana: N.C.T.E., 1990.

Britton, James, et al.. *The Development of Writing Abilities (11-18).* London: Macmillan Education, 1975.

Comely, Nancy R., and Robert Scholes. "Literature, Composition, and the Structure of English," *Composition and Literature: Bridging the Gap.* Ed. Winifred Bryan Horner. Chicago: University of Chicago Press, 1983. 96-109.

Woolf, Virginia. "'I Am Christina Rossetti,'" *Collected Essays.* Vol IV. New York: Harcourt, 1925. 54-60.

Figure 1

Some Questions about Virginia Woolf

1.   What do you make of "The Mark on the Wall"? Did you enjoy it? Did you understand it? Could you discern any structure, theme, or unifying point to it? Is it serious, or whimsical—or what?

2.   How effective is the fanciful story of Shakespeare's sister? ("A Room of One's Own" 2174-79) What is Woolf's point in telling it? Do you think this might have been the fate of a bright, ambitious woman in Shakespeare's time? How much have things changed?

3.   In the selection, "Professions for Women," Woolf takes up some issues we spoke of earlier when reading Mary Wollstonecraft and Florence Nightingale. What similarities and differences do you notice in Woolf's discussion? Do they indicate any progress in resolving these issues? Why, or why not?

4.   In "Professions for Women," Woolf claims that her biggest obstacle as a writer was not men, but "The Angel in the House" (2215). Who is this strange creature and why did she give Woolf so much trouble? Do artists today still have to deal with her, or has she been pretty well conquered?

5.   Woolf speaks of the problems of a woman "telling the truth about my own experiences as a body" (2217). Is it more difficult for women than for men to do this? Do men have any phantoms comparable to "The Angel in the House" (2215)? What might they be?

Figure 2

General Suggestions and Guidelines for Writing Projects

These may be research papers, creative works, critical studies, epistles to friends--use your imagination.

You may choose to take a creative or imaginative approach. For instance, you might want to write some poetry inspired by the readings. Or you could write a letter to a friend about "Christabel." You might want to turn one of the works into a play for junior high students. Or you could create a lesson plan for introducing Romantic poetry to sixth graders.

You may want to relate one of these works to events today. You could write a series of letters telling Mary Wollstonecraft how much impact her ideas have had upon our own time. What evidence can you see of William Wordsworth's ideas in modern life? How does the role of the church, in your experience, resemble or differ from that portrayed by William Blake?

Or you could identify some question, issue, or problem that has come up in class discussions and explore it more fully: What are some essential differences between Romantic and Victorian writings, and in which works do these differences show up?

When I read and grade these papers, I consider each onebindividually. Rather than apply a single standard to such diverse writings, I'll keep several broad considerations in mind:

- How much effort and energy appear to have gone into this?
- How much creativity, imagination, thought?
- How thorough an understanding of the literature does this paper show?
- Are ideas fully developed and explored or passed over superficially?
- Is the writer's purpose clear? Is it significant? Is it achieved?
- Is the paper well written in terms of its overall design, its language, its surface features of mechanics and usage?

Beyond the Great Wall of Language: The Early Poetry of Charles Wright

The Chinese say we live in the world of the ten thousand things,
Each of the ten thousand things
> *crying out to us*
Precisely nothing . . .

> —"Night Journal"

Wright's first book, *The Grave of the Right Hand* (1970), shows a fascination with beginnings and endings that continues in his later work. These points of starting and completion, however, are seldom clearly seen or explicitly pointed to, but are suggested indirectly in metaphor and symbol. Concrete, often sensuous images appear to emanate from and fade back into a remote source, at once personal and universal.

Beyond their engaging surfaces, the densely textured, allusive, and non-linear poems attempt to open and explore new realms of expressive possibility —unspoken and unwritten, like the "ditties of no tone" piped by the figures on Keats' Grecian urn.

To speak of symbolism in this sense is to focus on poetic imagination as mediator between the unknown and the known, reality as it may exist independent of human observation, and as it is transformed and constructed by human awareness. Such tenuous beginnings and endings, then, occur not in the first or last line of any individual poem or even in the succession of sharply-etched images, but in the resonance evoked by a particular conjunction of subject with object, knower with known.

Probing beyond surface impressions, as in "The Night Watch," the poems often call the very substantiality of objective phenomena into question:

The Night Watch

Outdoors, like a false morning,
Fog washes the pine trees. It
Shoulders against the windows,
Spreading across their surface
On its way upward. In this
Moment between sleep and thought

This holding back, I can hear
The fog start to rise, the slow
Memory of an ocean,
And I, like a ship, begin
To stir, to lurch in its swell,
And to move outward, beyond
The steel jetty, the lighthouse,
The red-flagged channel buoys,
—Beyond, at last, sleep even—

Into a deeper water,
Pale, oracular, its waves
Motionless, seagulls absent.

> Probing beyond surface impressions, . . . the poems often call the very substantiality of objective phenomena into question.

Fog washing the pine trees and spreading upward across the windows may be a precise, literal description of something actually observed, but this impression is undercut because the scene is "like a false morning," in which the fog, outside and pressing against the window, stirs an inner awareness, a "moment between sleep and thought," a twilight of consciousness in which the speaker no longer merely *sees* but actually *hears* the fog, and along with it, *hears* the "memory of an ocean" and begins to move "like a ship . . . into a deeper water,/Pale, oracular," a water clearly symbolic, an oracle, so that while "the steel jetty, the lighthouse, / The red-flagged channel buoys," maintain their sharp, imagist clarity, they are simultaneously immersed in a deeper imaginative context.

> Words become a way of opening the wall of conventional appearance to a place where language is not at home, yet where our experience of the world has its origin.

Fascination with this zone where perception begins and ends is especially evident in "The Bolivar Letters," a sequence of ten poems addressed to Tennessee's state institution for the insane. Number Eight, an adaptation from the French poet, Eugene Guillevec, likens this poetic *Abgrund* to a wall that must be hugged and finally opened with words:

8.

There are those who must speak,
Speak on from the shadow in the corners
About wounds which knit with much pain
On the clearest of nights;
And of ponds which yawn
In the face of a wall
That keeps them down in their beds.

There are those who must hug
This wall, this same wall,

And try to open it
With words, with names yet to be found
For that which has no form
And has no name.

Words become a way of opening the wall of conventional appearance to a place where language is not at home, yet where our experience of the world has its origin. Because language is both the means of opening this place and paradoxically an obstacle to entry, the poet gives a form and a name to the formless and nameless, all the while recognizing the presence of a something beyond, which remains formless and nameless. As Wright asks in "American Landscape":

What does one say? What can one say?
That death is without a metric,
That it has no metaphor?
That what will remain is what always remains:
The snow; the dark pines, their boughs
Heavy with moisture, and failing;
The clearings we might have crossed;
The footprints we do not leave?

Even as the poem affirms the power of language, it stresses the limits of language, juxtaposing the immediacy and palpability of natural phenomena with an awareness of how incomplete and inadequate any statement about what lies beyond this wall must be.

> Even as the poem affirms the power of language, it stresses the limits of language . . .

Hard Freight, Bloodlines, and *China Trace* form a trilogy with a dominant theme of uniting Wright's deeply felt personal history with an emerging poetic sensibility that draws heavily upon Italian and Oriental influences. Familiar themes from *The Grave of the Right Hand* remain central, but Wright's scope is enlarged by a growing inclusiveness, an increased awareness of the difficult poetic journey he has undertaken.

As though to underline both the expansion and the challenge, *Hard Freight* begins with an epigraph from Ezra Pound, the seminal and perhaps most important influence on Wright's poetry:

What is the use of talking, and there is no end of talking,
There is no end of things in the heart.

—*EP/Rihaku*

The quotation, from Pound's translation of Li Po's "Exile's Letter," offers a bridge between this book and the previous one. Still focused on language as both necessary and inadequate, it also foreshadows new directions, for while each book in the trilogy is distinctly individual, their overall progression reveals an evolution of theme and technique that cannot be fully seen in any one book. Among the qualities that emerge, and are forecast by the epigraph, are an increased sense of belonging to an ongoing poetic tradition; an increased influence of Pound, especially his syncretism and lineation; and perhaps most tellingly, the growing application of Oriental thought to Wright's dominant themes.

> Nevertheless, these influences do not appear to have penetrated deeply into a book whose heart and soul remain in Hardin County, Tennessee.

In *Hard Freight*, these tendencies are less pronounced than in the next two books. Beyond the epigraph, the book contains poems dedicated to Pound, Rimbaud, and Oscar Wilde, as well as to Baron Corvo and Abraham von Werdt, this last foreshadowing numerous later self-portraits in which Wright places himself in various imagined contexts. "Backtrack," with its "This is the death of water," echoes "The Waste Land," and Kafka's presence is invoked in "Homage to X" and "Entries." "Chinoiserie," the notes tell us, is based upon lines culled from *The Penguin Book of Chinese Verse*.

Nevertheless, these influences do not appear to have penetrated deeply into a book whose heart and soul remain in Hardin County, Tennessee. The voice of "Chinoiserie," for example, is both off-handed and eloquent, "Why not? The mouths of the ginger blooms slide open, . . ." Nor has Pound's influence at this point been deeply integrated into Wright's own style. Almost all of these poems, while written in free verse, are divided into regular stanzas, and in only two places (once in "Firstborn" and once in "Congenital") does Wright break a line visually, certainly a trademark of his later work. The book's strongest poems are not these excursions and experiments, however, but pieces like "One Two Three," "Dog Creek Mainline," "Blackwater Mountain," and especially "Northhanger Ridge," where sharp, clearly defined images sound the depths of memory and understanding in search of a center that can hold, a vision that will not dissolve.

Largely because of its controlling vision, *Bloodlines* is, in almost every way, stronger and more convincing than *Hard Freight*. At once more conservative and more ambitious, the collection is an affirmation of Wright's poetic and personal bloodlines. Pound is present, yes, but in a more subtle and integrated way—the resonance of an occasional image or turn of phrase, as "the acorn of crystal" in "Bays Mountain Covenant," echoing "Canto CXVI." Other presences also make themselves felt—Auden in "Delta Traveller," where "All this you survive, and hold on, / A way of remembering, a pulse," faintly echoes "In Memory of W. B. Yeats." Taken together, these moments suggest a growing sense of participation in a centuries-long conversation about being human, and a need on Wright's part to locate his voice, his experience, his vision, within that tradition. The subtle and fully integrated poetic allusions contribute resonance without undermining authenticity. Instead, they give notice that we are traveling in a certain sort of imaginative terrain.

The subtle and fully integrated poetic allusions contribute resonance without undermining authenticity.

The presence of Theodore Roethke can sometimes be felt in this way, in images of sod-lifting, bones, roots, and tendrils, and in the metaphor of skin as shell of the self. This is especially true of the long poem "Skins," an exploration of the relationship between identity and essence.

Number 6 is especially beautiful in its precise description of the metamorphosis of a mayfly, the emergence from water, the shedding of skin, the first experience of flight. All this, my fly fishing and biologist friends assure me, is a precise and accurate description of the mayfly's life cycle, compressed into a few beautiful lines. And also an apt metaphor for self-transformation:

6.

Under the rock, in the sand and the gravel run:
In muck bank and reed, at the heart of the river's edge:
Instar, and again instar,
The wingcases visible. Then
Emergence: leaf drift and detritus; skin split,
The image forced from the self.
And rests, wings drying, eyes compressed,
Legs compressed, constricted
Beneath the dun and the watershine—
Incipient spinner, set for the takeoff . . .
And does, in clean tear: imago rising out of herself
For the last time, slate-winged and many-eyed.
And joins, and drops to her destiny,
Flesh to the surface, wings on the slate film.

While the first few lines may recall Roethke, especially his *North American Sequence*, the language and imaginative perspectives have been internalized, even metamorphosed into Wright's unique way of seeing and speaking. The last line, for instance, with its four stresses, its strong medial caesura and balancing alliteration, calls up suggestions of Pound's adaptation of the Anglo Saxon stress-based line in "Canto I," but as with the Roethkean feel of the poem's opening, these overtones are subsumed by the poem's powerfully realized central image, which controls the overall effect.

In the third book of the trilogy, *China Trace*, Wright moves further from Hardin County and seems almost to wish to divest himself of his past, to undergo his own spiritual metamorphosis. As he says in "1975":

> *I open the book of What I Can Never Know*
> *To Page 1, and start to read:*
> *"The snow falls from the hills to the sea, from the cloud*
> *to the cloud's body, water to water . . ."*
> *At 40, the apricot*
> *Seems raised to a higher power, the fire ant and the weed.*
> *And I turn in the wind,*
> *Not knowing what sign to make, or where I should kneel.*

Epigraphs from Italo Calvino at the beginning of each book section imply that the world has become a book of emblems—a vast, intricate web of metaphor and symbol, in which surfaces are "skins." If this is an "Oriental" way of looking at experience, it is also, in many ways, very Western, suggesting especially the Italian neo-Platonists, the English metaphysicals, and the French symbolists. Hence perhaps, the book's name, *China Trace*—the hint of a trail or even bridge from the rich but somehow oppressive world of Kingsport, Tennessee, to a larger and more comprehensive sensibility. For this and other reasons, *China Trace* is a pivotal book. Marking the end of a trilogy, and in a larger sense of the first cycle of Wright's career, it ties together a number of threads that run through

If this is an "Oriental" way of looking at experience, it is also, in many ways, very Western, suggesting especially the Italian neo-Platonists, the English metaphysicals, and the French symbolists.

that early work, and at the same time suggests where his later work is headed.

The dominant persona is both Wright and not-Wright, a Bunyanesque Pilgrim on a spiritual journey from the known into the unknown. The book's overall movement can be seen by reading the first and last poems together. In "Childhood," Wright speaks in the first person, still very much a part of the life he sees himself leaving behind. His childhood is a dog that has followed him, and although its "beggar's lice" are still "bleaching to crystal along my britches leg," he's leaving, "tongue loosened, tracks apparent." He's found "a window into Away-From-Here, a place / I'm headed for." Unclear about where he is headed, perhaps because he doesn't know, he does tell what he is leaving behind—a catalogue of personal associations and Christian images.

> It is as though both personal history and conventional Christianity become mere husks or shells to be shed in the continuing metamorphosis of self.

Both of these motifs—transformation and departure—are implied in the "locust husk," which speaks on one level of a simple cicada shell, perhaps stuck to the side of a tree, and also recalls the theme of "Skins," especially the precise metamorphic description of "6." It is as though both personal history and conventional Christianity become mere husks or shells to be shed in the continuing metamorphosis of self.

"Him," the final poem, is written in the third person, as though Wright has at last become dissociated not merely from his childhood, but from himself, or more precisely, has become both subject and object, observer and observed:

Him

His sorrow hangs like a heart in the star-flowered boundary tree.
It mirrors the endless wind.
He feeds on the lunar differences and flies up at dawn.

When he lies down, the waters will lie down with him,
and all that walks and all that stands still, and sleep through
    the thunder.
It's for him the willow bleeds.
Look for him high in the flat black of the northern Pacific sky,
Released in his suit of lights,
            lifted and laid clear.

Now he flies. His sorrow, left behind like a locust shell, "hangs like a heart in the star-flowered boundary tree." He appears to have undergone the metamorphosis, transcended all sorrow, become the enlightened one. And perhaps "he" has, but the poem's speaker, someone very much like Wright, takes a jaundiced view of "his" triumph. Although "he" feels at harmony with the rhythms of nature and is "released," "lifted and laid clear," his lights are just a suit—not even skin, but some sort of artificial garment—while below him "his sorrow hangs like a heart . . . for him the willow bleeds," reminders of a world much more human and vital, but left behind.

Buddhism offers two very different models of the enlightened individual. One is the *Arhat*, who discovers the way to release from this world's endless cycle of suffering and pain, who lives his life so as to achieve that release, leaving behind the travail and heartache of other mortals. Another model is the *Bodhisattva*, who sees that same way but does not follow it, who chooses instead to remain *in* the world and *of* the world, to honor and experience the tragedies and triumphs of everyday life, yet to remind us of larger rhythms and deeper places.

> He appears to have undergone the metamorphosis, transcended all sorrow, become the enlightened one.

To point out this distinction and its relevance to *China Trace* is not to imply that Wright claims any special spiritual status for himself, but to suggest that the apparent turning away from the path of personal transcendence in "Him" need not be taken as a rejection of Eastern thought. In fact, *The World of the Ten Thousand Things*, which brings together the poems written since *China Trace*, takes its title from a Chinese expression that points to the paradoxical awareness that this world of everyday reality, for all its magnificent complexity and diversity, is somehow limited, just a part of the bigger picture.

If this bigger picture is fundamentally one of consciousness, that consciousness is not merely personal but universal and spiritual. What remains to be transcended, then, is not the physical world itself, but a certain limited way of being in that world, a way of seeing and of thinking. Thus, *The World of the Ten Thousand Things* affirms a commitment to the world of skins, mayflies, and locust shells, but also invokes a larger context that surrounds, embraces, and penetrates them.

> What remains to be transcended, then, is not the physical world itself, but a certain limited way of being in that world, a way of seeing and of thinking.

The World of the Ten Thousand Things, collects poems from *The Southern Cross* (1981), *The Other Side of the River* (1984), *Zone Journals* (1988), and *Xionia* (1990). Spanning a decade, the book invites discussion and reflection. Nevertheless, it is possible that the poetry will remain more often read than understood. As in "A Journal of True Confessions," lush imagery typically points to a remoter source: "The unseen bulking in from the edges of all things, / Changing the frame with its nothingness." To evoke a world beyond language has been an ongoing concern for Wright, however, and the earlier poems offer a useful context for reading *The World of the Ten Thousand Things*.

The opening poem of *The Southern Cross*, "Homage to Paul Cezanne," is a tribute to Cezanne as a painter, and at the same time an extended meditation on death, or more specifically on connections between the dead and the living. Wright speaks of the dead in lines that echo the epigraph from Li Po in *Bloodlines*:

Like us, they refract themselves. Like us,
They keep on saying the same thing, trying to get it right.

Mindful that the dead are remote if not inaccessible to the living, Wright asks:

Whose unction can intercede for the dead?
Whose tongue is toothless enough to speak their piece?

And replies:

What we are given in dreams we write as blue paint.
Or messages to the clouds.

In this reply, which emphasizes the need to write of "what we are given in dreams," something deeper and more remote than the dream itself, he recalls the poem's earlier imagery:

The dead are a cadmium blue.
We spread them with a palette knife in broad blocks and panes.
We layer them stroke by stroke
In steps and ascending mass, in verticals raised from the earth.
We choose and layer them in,
Blue and a blue and a breath,
Circle and smudge, cross-beak and buttonhook,
We layer them in. We squint hard and terrace them line by line.

While these lines speak of relations between the living and the dead, they also "layer in" a theory of composition—one that is associative, accumulative, and non-representational. The images are "smudged," "blurred," "layered," and "terraced." Squinting hard, "we choose and layer them in" "with palette knife in broad blocks and planes." If such images are representational at all, it is not in their photographic likeness to concrete, objective reality, but as mediators between "what we are given in dreams" and can only "write as blue paint." And precisely because "what we are given in dreams" is often refracted and hazy, we must keep on talking, "trying to get it right."

> The images are "smudged," "blurred," "layered," and "terraced." Squinting hard, "we choose and layer them in" "with palette knife in broad blocks and planes."

Other poems in *The Southern Cross* continue this layering and terracing of images. The visual, painterly orientation is apparent in several titles. Besides the five self-portraits, we find a "Portrait of the Artist with Hart Crane" and a "Portrait of the Artist with Li Po." We also find "Composition in Grey and Pink," "Spring Abstract," "Landscape with Seated Figure and Olive Trees," "Dead Color," and "Bar Giamaica," a poem inspired by a photograph. These titles, however, are only suggestive of the ways in which "Homage to Paul Cezanne" sets the tone for this collection. For instance, each self-portrait might be seen as a collage of images: at one moment the poet is "himself" looking out on the world, but he quickly jumps to an imagined "other" looking in on himself looking out. Taken individually, each poem presents a complex but apparently complete and finished portrait, yet taken together, each poem is merely a glimpse—partial, fragmented, isolated—of the whole self, which remains elsewhere.

The opening line from the book's title poem, "The Southern Cross," makes the point as clearly and directly as we are likely to find it, "Things that divine us we never touch." Although the word "things" calls to mind the title of this larger collection, *The World of Ten Thousand Things*, the word "divine" is more interesting in its ambiguity and thematic implications. Because "divine" is a verb, we are most likely to read it as meaning "discover," "locate," or "find out." How do "things" discover us, locate us, find us out? And who can read "divine" in the overall context of Wright's poetry without sensing the possible wordplay—not "discover," but "make holy" or "sanctify"? Can "things" make us holy, sanctify us? If so, how is it that we never "touch" them? How can mere "things" know us so intimately, define us and consecrate us, yet remain so elusive? This, finally, is the question that the book asks, as it tries to bridge the gulf between the seen and unseen worlds. Wright says in "Virginia Reel":

> It's worth my sighs
> To walk here, on the wrong road, tracking a picture back
> To its bricks and its point of view.
> It's worth my while to be here, crumbling this dirt through my
>   bare hands.
> I've come back for the first time in twenty years,
> Sand in my shoes, pockets full of the same wind
> That brought me before, my flesh
> Remiss in the promises it made then, the absolutes it's heir to.
> This is the road they drove on. And this the rise
> Their blood repaired to, removing its gloves.
> And this is the dirt their lives were made of, the dirt the world is,
> Immeasurable emptiness of all things.

If the world is dirt, if lives are dirt, this is a dirt that the speaker's bare hands like to crumble, perhaps as a part of the process of "tracking a picture back / To its bricks and its point of view." And if "things" themselves are finally empty, this emptiness is profound—infinite, beyond comprehension.

> How can mere "things" know us so intimately, define us and consecrate us, yet remain so elusive?

That everyday, quotidian reality is both mundane and ethereal, dirt-solid and spiritually elusive, is a central paradox of *The Southern Cross*, and indeed of this larger collection. In many ways, this refusal of transcendence, this commitment to the here and now, might be taken as the dominant theme of *The World of the Ten Thousand Things*. Even so, Wright's "here and now" is no longer just a narrow, shallow little place on the outskirts of Nirvanah. In its mystery, simplicity, complexity—reality and illusion—any place, any moment, can become

> Even so, Wright's "here and now" is no longer just a narrow, shallow little place on th eoutskirts of Nirvanah.

a two way mirror, doubling and reduplicating a dream, fracturing and extending an idea, throwing it back on its creator. Yet who is this watching from behind the glass—observing, judging, laughing, mocking, crying? Increasingly, the poetry focuses on the present, but the present grows deeper, more elusive, more numinous.

The title poem of *The Other Side of the River*, as though to continue this interpenetration of past with present, immediate with distant, opens at Easter among California palm trees but soon becomes a meditation on "the meta-weather of April." Besides recalling the rebirth archetype with all its Christian and pagan associations (including Eliot's *The Waste Land*), the poem fuses these with the Buddhist myth of the far shore. As recounted in Joseph Campbell's *Myths to Live By*: A pilgrim seeks passage from one side of the river, the world of daily reality, to the far shore—Nirvanah. Upon reaching this far shore, the pilgrim discovers a long line of people waiting for the same ferry to take them to Nirvanah, which they conceive to lie on the far shore, the land the pilgrim has just escaped. The point, of course, is that there is no "far shore," at least in the sense the pilgrim has imagined it. In connecting these Christian and Buddhist associations, Wright reaffirms his commitment to both traditions. Yet with characteristic modesty, he lays no claim to special spiritual insight.

Rather, he looks back twenty five years to another time when "anything I could think of was mine because it was there / in front of me, numinously everywhere." Then in a mood reminiscent of Henry Vaughan or Wiliam Wordsworth, he contrasts that childhood innocence with the present, "There comes a point when everything starts to dust away / More quickly than it appears, / when what we have to comfort the dark / Is just that dust, and just its going away." Or, in the poem's final stanza, "So to have come to this . . . / Is a short life of trouble." Whatever river he has crossed, the Savannah River or a more symbolic one, he finds himself still the person he has always been. Is this his rebirth, then—his metamorphosis? To come at last to a hard won acceptance of himself and his place on this earth?

> Is this his rebirth, then—his metamorphosis? To come at last to a hard won acceptance of himself and his place on this earth?

It would seem so, and yet the acceptance is accompanied by an enlarged vision that pays homage both to the numinosity of the everyday world and to the evocative power of human imagination:

> It's linkage I'm talking about,
>   and harmonies and structures
> And all the various things that lock our wrists to the past.
> Something infinite behind everything appears,
>   and then disappears.
> It's all a matter of how
>   you narrow the surfaces.
> It's all a matter of how you fit in the sky.

The ambiguity of the last line above is especially interesting in the way that it calls to mind two earlier poems. If "in" is read as shorthand for "into," the line offers an ironic reminder of "Him" from *China Trace*, in his "suit of lights." However, if the line is read to mean, "how you fit the sky in," it is more reminiscent of "Homage to Paul Cezanne," with its emphasis upon the terracing and layering of images. Either way, and both ways, it affirms a commitment to this world, a commitment made even more explicit in the last line of "Italian Days": "What gifts there are are all here, in this world."

Poems of *The Other Side of the River* range over and intertwine among Wright's characteristic subjects— country music, Italy, China, visual art. Much more than in *The Southern Cross*, the forms are open-ended and organic. The experiments with lineation, begun in *Hard Freight* and continued in subsequent books, are now features of Wright's style. In combining the longer, but dropped or broken lines with his collage-like layering of images he has evolved a style that is fragmented yet fluid, syncretistic yet connected. The underlying "harmonies and structures" that hold these poems together are easier to feel than to discuss, seeming sometimes to reside in the "something infinite behind everything" rather than the domain of rational discourse. The terrain of these poems is a world both known and unknown, a world of pieces and wholes, always present yet always, as in the last few lines of "California Dreaming," falling away:

> *Piece by small piece the world falls away from us like spores*
> *From a milkweed pod*
> *and everything we have known,*
> *And everyone we have known,*
> *Is taken away by the wind to forgetfulness,*
> *Somebody always humming*
> > *California dreaming . . .*

Given Wright's emphasis upon quotidian immediacy, it is perhaps not surprising that he would turn in *Zone Journals* and

> The experiments with lineation, begun in *Hard Freight* and continued in subsequent books, are now features of Wright's style.

Xionia to the journal as a poetic vehicle. With its off-handed, spontaneous feel and its improvisational juxtapositions, the journal would seem ideally suited to exploring this zone where event and imagination inform each other. In "Yard Journal," for instance, Wright appears to be letting his attention skip randomly from immediate sense impressions to the thoughts and feelings they evoke:

> —*Deep dusk and lightning bugs*
>   *alphabetize on the east wall,*
> *The carapace of the sky blue-ribbed and buzzing*
> *Somehow outside it all,*
> *Trees dissolving against the night's job,*
>   *houses melting in air:*
> *Somewhere out there an image is biding its time,*
> *Burning like Abraham in the cold, swept*
>   *expanses of heaven,*
> *Waiting to take me in and complete my equation:*
> *What matters is abstract, and is what love is,*
> *Candescent inside the memory,*
>   *continuous*
> *And unexpungable, as love is . . .*

All of these images—speculations—shift and dissolve into each other in a strange grammatical structure beginning with a dash and ending with an ellipsis. This is in many ways typical of these poems, which derive power from an underlying tension between the off-handed, extemporaneous feel of their movement and the deft assurance of Wright's maturing style. In much the same way, images and ideas presented matter-of-factly often reverberate back through earlier poems, placing familiar topics—shoes, rivers, dogs, red earth, retinas, the color blue—in new contexts, reconstituting and reconsidering them. Notice, for instance, how the penultimate stanza of "Journal of the Year of the Ox" hearkens back to and extends the imagery of "Homage to Paul Cezanne," merging it now with one of this poem's central images, the Blue Ridge, associated with the Battle of Island Flats, on the Holston River:

> *The pentimento ridgeline and bulk*
> *Of the Blue Ridge emerge*
> > *behind the vanished over-paint*
> *Of the fall leaves across the street,*
> *Cross-hatched and hard-edged, deep blue on blue.*
> *What is a life of contemplation worth in this world?*
> *How far can you go if you concentrate,*
> > *how far down?*

As the poems grow more associational and diffuse, their subject matter increasingly becomes the contemplative, meditative process itself. Apparently unrelated images and impressions rub against each other, disappear and reemerge in new surroundings, focusing their energy on the paradox of immateriality, the immeasurable emptiness of all things. Or as Wright puts it in "Night Journal II":

> *The breath of What's-Out-There sags*
> *Like bad weather below the branches,*
> > *fog-sided, Venetian*
> *Trailing its phonemes along the ground.*
> > *It says what it has to say*
> *Carefully, without sound, word*
> *After word imploding into articulation*
> *and wherewithal for the unbecome.*
> > *I catch its drift.*
>
> > · · ·
>
> *I long for clear water, the silence*
> *Of risk and of splendor,*

the quietness inside the solitude.
I want its drop on my lip, its cold undertaking.

Xionia in many ways represents an extension of the ideas and methods of *Zone Journals*. Although the collection itself and most poems within the collection are shorter and less wide-ranging than those in *Zone Journals*, Wright continues to use the poem/journal form, and he continues to focus on the life and process of contemplation.

More than in *Zone Journals*, however, he alludes to spiritual exemplars such as Richard of St. Victor, St. Augustine, St. Thomas, St. Jerome, Cold Mountain (Han Shan), Paul of Thebes, and Buddha. Here, too, he shows an increasing, almost metalinguistic, concern for the materials of poetic construction—parts of speech, morphemes, phonemes, individual letters. "Inaudible consonant inaudible vowel / The word continues to fall / in splendor around us," he says in "Silent Journal." "How can we trust the sure, true words / written in blue ink?" he asks in "A Journal of Southern Rivers." And in "Language Journal" he wonders, "What is it we can never quite put our fingers on / Inside the centricity of surface / that foregrounds and drains / the abstracts we balance our lives by? / Whatever it is, the language is only its moan."

For all of this hungering for a "something beyond," however, there is always a counterbalancing affirmation of this world's richness and complexity, a deep and abiding love for the people and places that have meant so much to him, an almost overwhelming sadness sometimes, at their inevitable passing. In "A Journal of Southern Rivers," he recalls a Montana summer:

Overcast, south wind,
Montana early July,
        fire in the barrel stove,
Bull thistle, yarrow and red clover
Adamant on the old trail.
Two jacksnipe scurry in single file across the yard.
One calls from the marsh.
Cold, rainy Thursday.
If being is Being, as Martin Heidegger says,
There is no other question,
        nothing to answer to,
That's worth the trouble.
In awe and astonishment we regain ourselves in this world.
There is no other.

Set against this affirmation, however, neither canceling it nor being absorbed by it, is an awareness spoken of in "Last Journal":

Last Journal

Out of our own mouths we are sentenced,
        we who put our trust in visible things.
Soon enough we will forget the world.
        And soon enough the world will forget us.
The breath of our lives passing from this one to that one,
Is what the wind says, its single word
        being the earth's delight.
Lust of the tongue, lust of the eye,
        out of our own mouths we are sentenced . . .

In his play upon the word "sentenced," suggesting both utterance and imprisonment, Wright gives concise expression to the fundamental tension running through *The World of the Ten Thousand Things* and evident in his earlier work as well. It is the tension we remarked earlier in number 8 of "The Bolivar Letters" from *The Grave of the Right Hand*:

There are those who must hug
This wall, this same wall,

And try to open it
With words, with names yet to be found
For that which has no form
And has no name.

Make It Online:
Writing and Teaching Poetry on the WWW

The bird, a nest. The spider, a web. Man, friendship.

—William Blake, A Proverb of Hell
from *The Marriage of Heaven and Hell*

A few years ago, a quick Google search for the word "poetry" took .06 seconds to return about 6,790,000 listings. Today that search took .10 seconds to return about 240,000,000 listings. It's hard to keep up. Unfortunately, I have not had time to review each of these sites, so I cannot offer a definitive assessment of the current state of poetry on the World Wide Web. No doubt the situation could be worse—and probably it could be much better. But clearly, huge numbers of people see the Web as a place to make, read, and discuss poetry. And they are doing just that. Who can stop them? Who would want to? Certainly not me.

> But clearly huge numbers of people see the Web as a place to make, read, and discuss poetry. And they are doing just that.

From a laptop computer in my basement in Boise, Idaho, with a Web browser and Internet connection, I can access, through sites like *Project Gutenberg* (http://www.guetenberg.org), the greatest literature ever written: *The Iliad*, *The Inferno*, *The Mahabharata*. And I can read contemporary poetry from Kabul, Dhaka, or Baghdad on sites not yet monitored, refereed, or hierarchically ranked by any official arbiters of poetic quality or political correctness. In this rapidly evolving literary medium, they exist alongside each other, woven together in a digital web, where they survive or perish based on their ability to build and hold a community of users.

And in a world with as much suffering and injustice as ours, we need poetry. Because poetry is the language of the human sprit—transcending political and sectarian barriers—it can become a powerful catalyst for transforming individual consciousness and global institutions, remaking our relationship to each other and to the planet, indeed even to the cosmos, a way, as William Carlos Williams has said, to "reconcile the people with the stones." Yes. And perhaps to reconcile the people with the people, an even more difficult task. True, we need food for the stomach, but we also need food for the spirit, for the imagination. Or, as Shelley puts it in his "Defense of Poetry":

> *The cultivation of those sciences which have enlarged the limits of the empire of man over the external world, has, for want of the poetical faculty, proportionally circumscribed those of the internal world; and man, having enslaved the elements, remains himself a slave.*

To more fully appreciate how this condition could apply to poetry and the World Wide Web, we might consider Alpha 60, a large, centralized electronic brain that monitors and regulates the populace in Jean-Luc Godard's 1965 film, *Alphaville*, which presents an ominous vision of a technocratic Utopia ruled by abstract reason, through appetite manipulation and saturation level social conditioning. The city of Alphaville is both a futuristic projection of what Paris, or Boise, might become in some distant time, like say 2011, and also a parallel or alternate dimension of reality, somewhere across "intersidereal space," a place where Mr.

True, we need food for the stomach, but we also need food for the spirit, and for the imagination.

Spock, chief science officer of Starship Enterprise, might feel very much at home.

As the film opens, our hero, Lemmy Caution, arrives from the Outlands in his new Ford Mustang and checks into a vast hotel. Part James Bond, part Humphrey Bogart, part Don Quixote, Caution is also part terrorist, before that word had its present associations. He has come to Alphaville on a mission. His goal? To take hostage or destroy Dr. Vonbraun, the creator of Alpha 60, thereby bringing down the mega-computer that is the controlling intelligence and digital soul of this megalopolis.

"Do you know what illuminates the night?" Alpha 60 asks Caution during his initial interrogation.

"Poetry," he replies, outwitting the machine.

Alphaville remains interesting today for the ways it both fails and succeeds as social prophecy. For instance, in portraying Alpha 60 as a giant, centralized "electronic brain" watched over by faceless geeks, the film misses what many see as the most significant development in computing between 1965 and the present: the growth of networking and distributed computing, specifically the Internet and the World Wide Web. Yet while this is not foreseen, the film does effectively project a future where technology is totally divorced from and at odds with human feelings, which have been exiled to the Outlands, and are hence regarded as dangerous, subversive, absurd, "outlandish." Feelings that cannot be demonized or repressed are sublimated into conventional and therefore non-threatening forms, or are commoditized and subsumed into the dominant technologic ethos.

In Alphaville, the Bible and the dictionary are one, and because the dictionary is tightly controlled by the state, discussing emotions and feelings is impossible. The feelings themselves have lost their legitimacy, becoming mere vestigial remnants of a primitive past. If the only language in which citizens can express the inner life is a state-sanctioned repertoire of clichéd expressions poured into specious, pseudo-rationalistic thought processes, freedom of expression is meaningless. How can we conceive what we cannot imagine? How can we express what we cannot conceive? Residents of Alphaville can think whatever they choose, but they cannot choose the unthinkable. Nor can they utter the unspeakable.

How can we conceive what we cannot imagine? How can we express what we cannot conceive?

In the course of Lemmy's search for Dr. Vonbraun, he encounters such a dilemma. Having resisted the advances of two class 3 seductresses, he meets and falls for Vonbraun's daughter, Natasha, and from then on divides his time about equally between trying to kill her father, a mission at which he eventually succeeds, and trying to convince Natasha that her emotions are real, especially the emotion of love, which she denies vigorously right up until the final scene in which the two escape Alphaville by fleeing to the Outlands not in Lemmy's Ford Mustang, but a commandeered Plymouth Valiant.

However close today's technocracies may be to such a society of mass cultural hypnosis, doublethink, and interminable war—and I sometimes think we are very close indeed—we would surely be much closer if not for poetry and the World Wide Web. Operating independently, each is a powerful force for individual growth and fulfillment; when combined, the resulting synergies can be liberating in ways that could not have been foreseen in 1965, and are only now becoming apparent.

The era of omnipotent, standalone master computers, like Alpha 60, has been superseded by the era of distributed networking, in which "The Network IS the computer." Suddenly and unexpectedly, computers can talk to each other, or more precisely, and this is crucial, people can talk to each other, even write to each other, through computers. As a result, we see what should have been apparent all along: computers are not malevolent, mutant machines at odds with everything human, but tools created by humans, for humans, to store, manage, and share information.

From the technology of the rock and chisel to that of the quill pen, to that of the typewriter, and finally the word processor is a long and profound journey, but in the end, despite technological transformations that impact every aspect of writing, we still have a writer, a text, and a reader. And in spoken communication, we have a similar progression, from speaking through megaphones and bullhorns, to landline phones, to today's digital handheld wireless devices that combine voice messaging, voice recognition, visual iconography, data storage, texting, and email in ways that defy easy categorization.

> Suddenly and unexpectedly, computers can talk to each other, or more precisely, and this is crucial, people can talk to each other, even write to each other, through computers.

As these technologies converge and spread, it becomes clear that among the most important functions of computers are memory and communication. In their SDRAM chips, in massive hard drives and removable flash drives and DVDs, computers are vast databanks. That much is obvious, but less often noted is the fact that those bits and bytes of information contain not just Social Security numbers and train schedules, but music, movies, emails, articles, photos—and yes, fiction and poetry. True, the amount of fiction and poetry contained in digital format represents a tiny proportion of the total data stored on computers worldwide, but the literature already online shows the potential of digital media as a literary resource, a vast electronic library where readers can find the poetry of Rabindranath Tagore, or Issa, or Charles Baudelaire, or Denise Levertov from anywhere on earth with the click of a mouse. And this movement cannot be stopped by Alpha 60, or any other force I am aware of, though some would very much like to.

More literature comes online all the time, as writers unlock the communication potential of digital media. Poets are learning that computers are useful not only as standalone word processors, but as publishing tools and community builders. Through labyrinthine passageways of cables and hubs and routers and keyboards and monitors, today's computers connect writers and readers around the world. As these trends become ever more pronounced, the privileging of printed text over digital text becomes harder to justify.

If a poet composes on a keyboard, or with voice-recognition software, then transmits that message electronically—perhaps as an email, perhaps as a web page, perhaps as a file attachment—the recipient can interact with the poem in ways not available with the printed word. One way is, of course, to print the text, or to print some part of it. Or the recipient might open an attached file, edit it, re-attach it to an email, and send it on to another reader, who would also have several choices about how to interact with the work, thereby giving new meaning to Baudelaire's lines, quoted at one point by Lemmy Caution, *"Hypocrite lecteur, mon semblable, mon frere,"* for distinctions between writer and reader are

And this movement cannot be stopped by Alpha 60, or any other force I am aware of, though some would very much like to.

increasingly blurred in such scenarios, as are distinctions between written and spoken communication, or distinctions between the literary arts and the visual arts, especially if the medium is hypertext.

Through my website, *Paradigm Online Writing Assistant* (http://www.powa.org/), I have come to appreciate the political implications of the Web's global reach and also the ways this fluid and dynamic digital literary environment reconstructs relations of writer and reader in producing and consuming texts, as hitherto unimagined literary contexts emerge. But let me give a brief example.

In 1985, I published a writing textbook with a prestigious Boston publishing house. After a rigorous peer-review and editing process, the book came out. It was adopted at a few universities in the United States and Canada, but not enough to satisfy the publisher, who quickly backlisted it and let it go out of print. Fortunately, especially in those days, I had a digital version of the book, which I used to make handouts for my classes and continued to revise. In the early 1990s, before graphical Web browsers, I converted the text to run digitally in the background of WordPerfect 5.1, a DOS program, through a series of macros. Then, with the advent of Windows, I reconverted the book to hypertext as a Windows Help File. In both of these versions, the words took on a digital life (I lost track of pagination, of a sense of a linear beginning and ending, etc.), but in both cases, also, distribution was largely restricted to a small group of students via floppy disk. In the mid 1990's as graphic web browsing became more commonplace, I learned HTML, and right here in Paris, in 1996, at the Fifth World Wide Web Conference, I had a vision of how I could convert this proprietary, static, standalone Windows Help

File into a platform independent, scalable, distributed web of hyperlinked documents. With some difficulty, I did that, and published the results to my university's Web server, with no East Coast publisher, no peer review, no fanfare, no cash advance.

Eventually, the site moved off campus and gained its own domain name. It has been revised numerous times, in overall design and in the details of specific sections. For instance, users can download the entire text, which exists as a PDF file on the site, for use without a Web connection. I have published the site contents as an on-demand printed book. And I have added discussion forums in which users modify the site by adding questions and comments of their own. In intervening years, the site has won numerous awards and has had several million unique visitors from almost every country on Earth.

> According to Marko, the work was popular with its new audience, but unfortunately, the story does not end at this happy juncture.

Because my contact information is posted on the site, I often hear from users, writing to say thanks or to get help with a download. One such user was Marko Popovic, a lecturer at the University of Belgrade during the Milosovic era. He wanted to translate *Paradigm* into Serbian and publish and distribute it to teachers throughout what was then Yugoslavia. Of course, I agreed. And shortly thereafter, I began to receive *Svet Reci*, or *World of Words*, containing excerpted sections of *Paradigm* in a language, even an alphabet, I could not begin to read. According to Marko, the work was popular with its new audience, but unfortunately, the story does not end at this happy juncture.

I received one final communiqué from him. It reads, in part, as follows:

> It inspires me because it reaffirms my belief that words and ideas are important, that they do make a difference, that they stand in opposition to repressive authoritarian institutions that maintain themselves by rigid thought control and enforced ignorance.

. . . you were addressee of letters that were written by my fingers and 'colleagues' Jasmina _____, syntaction, and Ljiljana _____, pedagogyst, escorted by others, in other words by unwelcomed non-professionals in the field. Also, my email was constantly supervised by mentioned people. I don't intend to burden you further than this with my personal and professional problems, but I want to fill the other half of the content with my conscientious self now when I feel to be left alone for a while. Today, after years of pondering, I resigned from my job at University of Belgrade and I decided not to publish the articles submitted for Svet Reci *No 5 for, now I see with myself, lots of reasons. Many of them are to deal with claustrophobiac, xenophobiac and homophobiac culture.*

Fortunately, it is likely Paradigmica *to see the light with non governmental publications, but before I get idea how to realize it, I shall first have to seriously heal myself after several months of putting up with torture by national 'psychoanalysists'. Once again, I am sorry, and I hope that stream in this once upon a time cosmopolitan city won't go further on in their destruction, not further than me and the mentioned method.*

Sincerely Yours,

Marko Popovic

Although I have tried to contact Marko since then, that was the last I heard from him, and it saddens me to think that my work, and Marko's commitment to inquiry, learning, language, and communication—embodied in this case by his translation and dissemination of my writing—may have led in part to his persecution by the authorities of the Alphaville that was Belgrade in 1999. It saddens me, and yet it inspires me. It inspires me because it reaffirms my belief that words and ideas are important, that they do make a difference, that they stand in opposition to repressive authoritarian institutions that maintain themselves by rigid thought control and enforced ignorance.

Besides *Paradigm*, my Web efforts have focused on three other areas: my classes at Boise State University, a website I designed for the Log Cabin Literary Center, and *poetryexpress* (http://www.poetryexpress.org/), which debuted in August of 2001. This site offers inspiration, guidance, and instruction in writing, reading, and discussing poetry.

In my teaching, I use Web sites to supplement traditional on-campus classes and also as standalone online classes. In 2002, for instance, I have two different on campus courses in session. One is a literature course and the other a writing course. While I am here in Paris, both are doing a series of online activities on their class websites. In the British literature course, students are exploring the online companion site to their textbook and also the *Victorian Web*, and are conducting a web-based discussion in which I can participate while I'm physically here in France. In my writing class, students are having an online writing workshop, where they post drafts of their essays and comment on their classmates' drafts. Again, I can drop in on the workshop from any place in the world that has an Internet connection. In the fall, this writing website will be upgraded a bit and used to teach a completely online version of the same class.

> In my writing class, students are having an online writing workshop, where they post drafts of their essays and comment on their classmates' drafts.

The Log Cabin Literary Center is a local, community-based, non-profit organization whose mission is as follows: "We exist to inspire & celebrate a love of reading, writing & discourse throughout the region." They fulfill this mission by sponsoring a visiting writers series, a summer writing camp, a writers in the schools program, as well as readings, workshops, writing groups, and book discussion groups. Their website is used primarily to communicate with local members about upcoming events and activities, and also to showcase their programs. Additionally, the site gives them national and international exposure, but its primary purpose is to enhance and complement their local and regional mission.

> As in so many other areas, William Blake is an inspiration here ... mainly for the audaciously liberating imagination at the heart of his work.

Since going online in 2001, my most recent site, *poetryexpress*, has had millions of unique visitors from around the world. As in so many other areas, William Blake is an inspiration here, for his comment on webbing in *The Marriage of Heaven and Hell*, of course, but also for his ingenious blendings of poetry and visual iconography, for his mastery of juxtaposition and nonlinear structure, but mainly for the audaciously liberating imagination at the heart of his work.

The underlying philosophy of *poetryexpress* is implicit in the following passage from the site itself:

> *Making poems must be among the most natural and primitive human activities. For while it's true that composing poetry, like dancing or singing, rewards dedicated study and practice, we are all poets to some extent, especially when we feel our language open new ways of imagining and seeing. . . . Like inhaling and exhaling, like listening and speaking—sharing and making poems are two parts of a larger process.*

When we read or hear poetry, we absorb words, images, ideas, fresh perspectives, new insights. When we discuss or write poetry, we invigorate an ancient tradition that constantly evolves and reshapes itself. . . . The more poetry you read, write, and discuss, the more you'll appreciate the range of possibilities open to you. And your understanding of life, of what it is to be human, will keep growing, too.

Key site components include "E-Muse," a text-generating engine that uses Flash technology to construct poems from random words supplied by users. Another section, "15 Poems You Can Write Now," is a collection of activities to help aspiring poets generate poems using formal and conceptual schemata. A representative activity, "Talk to animals (and stars)," focuses on the apostrophe and includes William Blake's, "The Tyger," and several other poems as models for discussion and emulation.

Another section, "Write a one-sentence poem," includes William Carlos Williams' "The Red Wheelbarrow" and John Keats' "Bright star, would I were steadfast as thou art" as examples. "Tips & Techniques" is a concise, practical guide to such topics as "Figurative Language" and "Harmonic Texture." These topics are linked to numerous definitions and include poetic examples from traditional favorites and contemporary writers—even one of my own poems.

An important feature of *poetryexpress* is its emphasis on composing, which is broken into four stages—making, sharing, revising, and publishing. The pedagogy here blends a traditional writing workshop model with recent research

on composing processes. Students first generate drafts of
their poems, then share their drafts in peer response groups
following the "No Praise/No Blame Method," as described on
the site. Having given and received feedback on their work,
students then revise it and finally publish it in traditional
print media, in a classroom publication, or in digital form at
an appropriate venue on the Web, and there are many.

Because the site is scalable, it can keep growing. Over the
next few years, I hope to add several components. Among
these could be poetry competitions,
more sophisticated text generating
engines, discussion groups, publication
opportunities, as well as audio and
video enhanced pages, like those at
the *Favorite Poem Project* (http://
www.favoritepoem.org/), a successful
American site that has enormous
possibilities for diversification and
global development.

> For there is no escaping that the same globalizing tendencies we see operating in the world of trade and finance are also at work in the arts and humanities.

As a result of these experiences, I am convinced that the
Internet, especially the World Wide Web, offers artists and
humanists a powerful new medium for self-expression and for
helping to shape the social and political transformations that
will inevitably occur in this era of globalization. For there is no
escaping that the same globalizing tendencies we see operating
in the world of trade and finance are also at work in the arts
and humanities. And we in the arts and humanities must take
advantage of the Web to build international communities
of readers and writers. This conference itself could be cited
as evidence that such a movement is underway, as could the
global writing communities established by trAce.

When I review statistics from my websites and see visitors
from Iceland, Pakistan, Ecuador, Zaire, Sri Lanka, Yemen,
and Somalia, I have a greatly enlarged sense of mission,

purpose, and responsibility. And when these international visitors become more than just statistics, as was the case with Marko, I am forced to rethink the personal, social, and political implications of my work in a global context. For just as economic globalization can be a mixed bag of material wealth purchased at the cost of individual dignity, environmental destruction, and local cultural autonomy, so can the dominance of the English language and of Eurocentric values, propounded intentionally or not, devalue, drown out, and ultimately silence the local indigenous voices of others who do not have access to the same base of intellectual and technological capital as those whose cultures dominate the international stage. It is essential to tread lightly, to listen, to consider, and to enable others through two way communication and through efforts to bridge the digital divide by providing educational and technological empowerment to those whose voices are not being heard.

Yet while literary web building clearly has profound political implications, it does not and cannot have a specific political agenda. Certainly, individual writers will have strongly held personal and political convictions, which will inform their writing and web building. If not, why write? But in this distributed digital environment the keynotes will always be individuality and diversity, negotiation and collaboration. In chat rooms, listservs, and bulletin boards, one way information dissemination is transformed into polyvocal discussion and conversation. In contrast with the univocal, centralized, hierarchical communication structure of conventional mass media, the Internet thrives on diversity and interactivity.

> In contrast with the univocal, centralized, hierarchical communication structure of conventional mass media, the Internet thrives on diversity and interactivity.

But for all the changes wrought by the Web, some things have not changed. Poets among us retain their ancient mandate to stir and enlighten the spirit by giving form to our unvoiced needs and yearnings. What is new is the chance to use this astoundingly powerful new communication technology of the Internet to redeem and remake our wounded planet's literary consciousness, to illuminate the night while truly doing "things unattempted yet in prose or rhyme."

Linking the Humanities Across Space and Time

Maybe—well, almost certainly—I've been online too much lately. I'm seeing links everywhere. It's just a click from "Beowulf in Hypertext" a resource on the Anglo Saxon epic, to *beowulf.org*, a project of Scyld Software, which seeks "to determine the applicability of massively parallel computers to the problems faced by the Earth and space sciences community." Because of the Web—even when I'm offline—my thinking is more associational, digressive, serendipitous, less linear. Like Kurt Vonnegut's Billy Pilgrim, I leap from time to time and place to place, if not physically at least in my imagination, in my teaching and writing.

I turn away from the computer screen for a glance at my notes. It's 7:20 a.m., and I'm in my office sipping coffee before class, Survey of British Literature I, where in about twenty minutes, we'll be starting *Beowulf*, that ancient tale of heroic valor, tribal vengeance, dragon slaying, feasting hall and funeral pyre, clashings of good and evil. Originally composed in an oral tradition and sung by a bard at ceremonial occasions, this tribal epic was transcribed in the eighth century and then passed down in print over a millennium, over an ocean, to us upstairs in room 203, LA BLDG, to fill a few hours for students needing three core credits as part of the humanities requirement, on the way to a bachelor's degree, a ticket to success in "the real world."

> Because of the Web—even when I'm offline—my thinking is more associational, digressive, serendipitous, less linear.

Beowulf comes early in the term, after "Caedmon's Hymn" and "The Wanderer," two short and fairly accessible pieces that help give us a feel for Anglo Saxon culture and poetry. *Beowulf* is longer, more complex and more demanding. Fortunately, we have a stunning new verse translation by Seamus Heaney, the Nobel Prize winning contemporary poet from Northern Ireland. Heaney brilliantly captures the alliterative, stress-based rhythms of the original poem in phrasing that is fresh and accessible to twenty-first century ears.

In his Introduction to his translation, Heaney notes that

. . . for reasons of historical suggestiveness, I have in several instances used the word "bawn" to refer to Hrothgar's hall. In Elizabethan English, bawn (from the Irish bó-dhún, a fort for cattle) referred specifically to the fortified dwellings which the English planters built in Ireland to keep the dispossessed natives at bay, so it seemed the proper term to apply to the embattled keep where Hrothgar waits and watches.

> Heaney brilliantly captures the alliterative, stress-based rhythms of the original poem in phrasing that is fresh and accessible to twenty-first century ears.

Seen from such a perspective, Heorot, the lofty house of the Ring Danes, comes to look more and more like a colonial garrison and Grendel and his mother like dispossessed natives. Taking our cue from Heaney, we speculate how this poem might help us understand the "troubles" of Northern Ireland, the conflicts between European settlers and Native Americans, or the attacks of 9/11 on the World Trade Center and the Pentagon—

*So after nightfall, Grendel set out
for the lofty house, to see how the Ring-Danes
were settling into it after their drink,
and there he came upon them, a company of the best
asleep from their feasting, insensible to pain
and human sorrow. Suddenly then
the god-cursed brute was creating havoc:
greedy and grim, he grabbed thirty men
from their resting places and rushed to his lair,*

flushed up and inflamed from the raid,
blundering back with the butchered corpses.

Even so far from its original context in time, place, and language, the poem is a pleasure to read aloud, and students enjoy hearing it, so I alternate the reading of selected passages with twenty-minute mini-lectures and class discussions. We study the poem's language, its structure and design, its dominant themes and images, its historical context and possible contemporary analogues. As Heaney says, "Putting a Bawn into *Beowulf* seems one way for an Irish poet to come to terms with that complex history of conquest and colony, absorption and resistance, integrity and antagonism . . .."

Beowulf, in Heaney's translation, almost teaches itself, even at 7:40 a.m. I'd like to stick with it, but this is a survey class. We've got a lot of literature to cover this term, far too much really; and after a week and a half it's time to move on to other works, like *The Book of Margery Kempe*, a lively and moving spiritual narrative by a fourteenth century mother of fourteen, an independent-minded woman who went into business and became one of the most successful brewers in Norfolk. Overcome by deep spiritual longings, however, she takes a vow of chastity and wins her husband's consent to embark on a religious pilgrimage to Jerusalem. Before departing, she seeks counsel from the anchoress, Dame Julian of Norwich, who tells her,

> Set all your trust in God and fear not the language of the world, for the more despite, shame, and reproof that ye have in the world, the more is your merit in the sight of God.

On her pilgrimage Kempe develops a deep sense of compassion for the sufferings not just of humans but of animals:

And . . . if she saw a man had a wound or a beast, . . . or if a man beat a child before her or smote a horse or another beast with a whip, . . . her thought she saw our Lord be beaten or wounded . . ..

On returning home, she begins preaching her unorthodox faith of compassion and is eventually brought before the powerful Archbishop of York, who calls her a Lollard and a heretic; but in the end her persistence and sincerity win his blessing.

> Adjuncts are by definition "nonessential," a fact of which they are regularly reminded by their pay, their lack of job security, and their general working conditions.

Margery Kempe wasn't an author we studied when I was a student, but I'm grateful for the research of Sanford B. Meech and Hope Emily Allen, who discovered and edited the tale of this most extraordinary woman. Although different from *Beowulf* in many ways, Kempe's story also derives from an oral tradition and was told to a scribe who was able to capture on paper much of the spontaneity and idiomatic freshness of her everyday speech.

Before coming to Boise State University in 1981, I taught as an adjunct instructor at Kansas State University. Adjuncts are by definition "nonessential," a fact of which they are regularly reminded by their pay, their lack of job security, and their general working conditions. Much of my teaching during those years was done in night classes at Fort Riley, home of the 1st Infantry, the Big Red One. Because hardly anyone else, including most of the adjuncts, wanted to go there, I was given all sorts of courses that I would never have had a shot at on campus—Humanities: Classical; Humanities: Baroque & Enlightenment; and Humanities: Modern.

We studied the love poems of Sappho, the epics of Homer. Read *Agamemnon* and *Oedipus Rex*. Learned about "entablature" and "frieze." "Ionic." "Corinthian." "Doric." Typically, the humanities class would be taught in a two-hour session Monday and Wednesday evenings from 6:00 to 8:00, back to back with another class that met from 8:00 to 10:00. On Tuesday and Thursday this pattern was repeated.

My second preparation was English Composition, an area I had never formally studied. Like most instructors I pieced these composition courses together from the English Department's teaching guide, occasional staff meetings, and memories of my own freshman comp experience. I recall a colleague suggesting that I think for a while about the truly outstanding teachers I'd had—the ways they'd inspired, challenged, and supported me. That was good advice. As my mind replayed favorite classes I'd taken—German, with Herr Rothfuss; Advanced Writing, with Ken Macrorie; Chaucer, with James Sledd; Milton, with William P. Williams —I recalled diverse techniques and teaching styles, and the one common thread running through them all: the teachers' deep love for their subjects and their eagerness to inspire that love in their students.

> I recall a colleague suggesting that I think for a while about the truly outstanding teachers I'd had—the ways they'd inspired, challenged, and supported me.

My Fort Riley students could always bring me back from such lofty soaring. For the most part, they were enlisted personnel and dependants, sometimes retired military. By day they trained or worked, often in clerical or equipment maintenance positions, and by class time they were tired but ready for a change. Students from a 6 p.m. humanities class would often reappear in an 8 p.m. composition class, so I could blur the borders a bit and link some of the content. For instance, if we'd been discussing Plato and Aristotle in humanities and studying argument in composition, I could bring some classical rhetoric into the writing class. Once while leading into a unit on argument, I was trying to explain the meaning of the word "rhetoric" and somehow came up with the hypothetical example of two people arguing over possession of a cow in a time before courts or lawyers. This led to a discussion that went, as best I can reconstruct it, as follows:

> "Why, that one damn chicken could cost you a whole month's pay."

"You know," said Maynard, "what you just said about that cow makes me think of France back in World War II when I was there and they did it there. If you were in a jeep, say, and you hit a chicken, I mean run over it, and they all came out of their houses and take you to court, you have to pay not just for the chicken, but they figure way back to how old he is and how many years he's got left and how many eggs he might lay and then they give you the bill. Why, that one damn chicken could cost you a whole month's pay."

"Yep that's how it is," Maria agreed. "Even in Hungary we have it the same and in Germany, too."

"When I was in Germany," Danny put in, "I saw this guy drive a half-track out in a field and rip it all up and they charged him a thousand dollars, and hell, the farmer was right over there plowin' it up anyhow, and they charged him a thousand dollars. Course it did get pretty bad sometimes. I mean I remember they had these big white posts alongside the road, and we'd just drive along and mow 'em down for the hell of it."

"Good times," I said, trying to shake the class loose from the spell that had fallen over us all. "Well," I continued, searching for a link back to something I might have said about a cow, "That's what those Sophists were like, or so Socrates says. They didn't care about what was right or wrong or true or false, just as long as they got what they wanted. They didn't care about the truth, just about winning the case."

"Sounds like my husband," Maria said, "All he does is argue. At home. At a meeting. At work."

"A born rhetorician," I put in.

"That's for sure. He really is. He comes home and walks in from work and says, 'Hey, what's with all the rhetoric around here?'"

"Okay then, let's look at Martin Luther King's rhetoric in 'Letter From Birmingham Jail,' page 628."

"Who says a person can't be a radical and still be patriotic?" Danny interjected suddenly. "What about Socrates? What about King?"

"Was King a radical? Was Socrates? Were they patriotic? Let's consider this. Let's look at King's letter."

But that discussion happened a long time ago, in another state. For the past twenty three years, I've lived and taught in Idaho, and for the past five years, I've served on the IHC's Board of Directors, an honor and responsibility that has also been a lot of fun. IHC's stated mission of "deepening understanding of human experience by connecting people with ideas," involves a variety of efforts to carry humanistic learning beyond the classroom. Besides sponsoring an annual Distinguished Humanities Lecture and Dinner that brings internationally known speakers to Idaho, we have our own IHC Speakers Bureau, which sends Idaho humanities scholars to lecture throughout the state; and we offer grants to public school teachers, to museums and libraries, and to other individuals and institutions with ideas for innovative public programming in the humanities.

"Who says a person can't be a radical and still be patriotic?" Danny interjected suddenly.

On February 22, 2003, IHC held a ceremony to honor Horace Axtell, a Nez Perce elder, for Outstanding Achievement in the Humanities. His extended family was there—wife, children, grandchildren, nieces, nephews—along with many others who have been influenced by his efforts to preserve his tribe's language and culture and build bridges of understanding to the dominant culture.

Axtell's book, *A Little Bit of Wisdom*, is part memoir, part tribal history, and part spiritual reflection. Like *Beowulf* and *The Book of Margery Kempe*, it comes out of an oral tradition. Axtell was assisted by Lewiston writer, Margo Aragon, who taped and transcribed his reminiscences and observations then shaped them into a book, while maintaining his distinctive voice and style. As Axtell tells stories of his Christian upbringing, his military service during WWII, his brief time in prison afterward, and his battles with alcohol, one dilemma he constantly returns to is his struggle to live simultaneously in two different cultures, while not feeling truly a part of either.

> Finally, he comes to accept and embrace his cultural heritage, including the Seven Drum Religion, or *walahsat*, which, as a younger man, he had been taught to reject as heathen.

All of this, and especially his time in the military, leads him to consider how the "united" in United States might apply to his people: "I don't think it means that we should forget our own ways or our own language. We're of a different race, a different color, a different breed, and we can't ever get away from that." Finally, he comes to accept and embrace his cultural heritage, including the Seven Drum Religion, or *walahsat*, which as a younger man he had been taught to reject as heathen. As he puts it, "The life we have is the life we want to hold on to—our Indian ways. These ways were left here from our old people. Our ancestors done it that way, one heart to the other. It's still here. You can trace it back."

At the award ceremony in Lewiston there was drumming and chanting. Many people stood and spoke about Horace Axtell, telling stories, offering anecdotes and memories. For some speakers, a certain shyness or reticence clearly made this difficult. A few made their way to the microphone in wheelchairs. One, clinging to a walker, joked that her Indian name means "Traveling Woman." Tears were held in check as long as possible, then released and transformed into laughter. Hugs were exchanged. The Nez Perce and English languages commingled and harmonized.

> Tears were held in check as long as possible, then released and transformed into laughter. Hugs were exchanged. The Nez Perce and English languages commingled and harmonized.

Then, as the tributes ended and the drumming began again, an honor guard of Nez Perce military veterans took up the colors and marched slowly and solemnly, Indian style, almost a shuffle really, from the front of the room to stand by the drumming circle—at least three, maybe four generations standing there, until with a solid thump at the end of the rising, winding voices, the ceremony ended.

Margo Aragon summed up my feeling at that moment pretty well when she wrote, "To be around Horace is to step into a place where time and space are meaningless words. The past becomes the present and the future unrolls before your eyes."

It's a feeling I get a lot these days, an intriguing riddle that's hard to put into words. T. S. Eliot comes close to articulating the sensation at the start of his poem "Burnt Norton" when he writes,

Time present and time past
are both perhaps present in time future,
and time future contained in time past.

So at least I'm not alone in this nonlinear, associational sense of time. Events, words, and images from the present are woven with visions of the past and the future into a single fabric. And apparently the Internet isn't entirely to blame. It could be due partly to the humanities.